THINGS FOUND WHERE?

Every Chapter in the Bible Described with Hundreds of Quotable Quotes and Sentence Sermons

Thomas J. Knickerbocker

Faithful Life Publishers
North Fort Myers, FL
FaithfulLifePublishers.com

Foreword

As I was previewing "That's Found Where?" it occurred to me that the man who wrote this had an excellent working knowledge of the Bible. When one considers that there are two Testaments with 66 Books and 1189 chapters, that is no small order. Tom Knickerbocker is the man with that insight.

So, "Who is Tom Knickerbocker?" one might say. He is the son of a preacher and the brother of three preachers and a deacon. He has pastored Baptist Churches, been a Christian educator, and has been involved in world-wide missions, conducting American missions conferences and taking mission trips to Africa. Brother Knickerbocker has authored a number of books on the Christian life and has been a newspaper columnist with a local paper dealing with issues of the day.

The value of this book is two-fold. First, it can be used to survey all the chapters of a given book in the Bible; and second, it can be used as a review of a given book, bringing to mind the contents of the chapters. For an example, in the entry under "Genesis 2" there is "More details on Creation; God creates man, woman and marriage." That can be used as a survey and/or a review.

Also the sentence quotes from the Bible and sermons under the chapter headings are an added blessing to this volume. My life's verses are Psalm 119:161, 162 "Princes have persecuted me without a cause; but my heart standeth in awe of thy word. I rejoice at thy word, as one that findeth great spoil." I recommend this book to all who have a love for God's Word.

Don Strange, Pastor
Winkler Road Baptist Church
Fort Myers, Florida

Table of Contents

Introduction

Throughout my over 35 years in the ministry, I have had the privilege of preaching from every book of the Bible. Yet, I struggled with finding certain passages from memory, especially in the gospels; such as the Parable of the Sower, certain miracles of Christ, etc. As a result I spent a couple of years studying and writing down a synopsis of the contents of each chapter of each book of the Bible. If I knew the general area of the passage I was searching for, I could find it much easier by looking at my study and identifying the details I desired. It has been an aid in my sermon preparation and personal Bible study. Perhaps it will be a blessing to you, the reader, as well.

Then, sometime later as I was doing my daily Bible reading, I noticed numerous quotes I had jotted down in the margins of my Bible taken from preaching I had heard or personal observations I had written down myself. "Sentence Sermons," you might say, or we could call them "Bible Bits and Bytes." Finally, I wrote down the over 300 statements linking them to the chapter and verse(s) to which they applied. The names of those I quoted were the ones I heard say them. The quotes not labeled are those of speakers I failed to write down or those which were original. The verse reference that follows each quote identifies the place in that respective chapter from where the quote comes. Each quote is in italics to differentiate it from the chapter summary.

The thought occurred to me to put the two studies together which would not only give a synopsis of each chapter, but also provide helpful illustrations for pastors, teachers or anyone interested in knowing their Bible better. I trust that this resource will be a great addition to the reader's library providing reference material for more effective ministry.

The title of the book was suggested by my good friend Dr. Don Strange, pastor of Winkler Road Baptist Church in Fort Myers, Florida. It encapsulates the very reason for the book. Much thanks to my wife, Barbara and Pastor Simon Watts of Manchester, England for their help in editing the text.

Thomas J. Knickerbocker

GENESIS

1. Six days of creation.

2. More detail on the creation; God creates man, woman and marriage.

3. The Fall of man into sin.

"You can choose to sin,
but you cannot choose the consequences." v. 6-7

4. Cain and Abel; Descendants of Cain; Birth of Seth.

"Satan was rebellious against the position of God,
Adam against the commandment of God,
and Cain against the plan of God." Ch. 3,4

5. Descendants of Seth to Noah.

6. Sons of God sin; Noah builds Ark.

7. God floods the earth.

8. Noah exits Ark and worships.

9. Human government instituted; Canaan is cursed.

10. The Table of Nations from sons of Noah.

11. Tower of Babel; Descendants of Shem to Abraham.

"When God is in it, our weakness becomes strength;
but when God is not in it,
our strength becomes weakness." v. 1-9

12. God chooses Abraham; He lies about his wife in Egypt.

"ALTAR: *Admission, Listen for direction, Transformation, Adoration,*
Rejoicing" - Eldon Stevens
Gen. 12:7,8; 13:4,18; 22:9-14
"The world takes note when a believer sins." v. 18

13. Abraham and Lot separate; God's promise of the land.

14. Abraham delivers Lot; He meets Melchizedek.

15. God's promise to Abraham of a son and land.

16. Abraham, Hagar and Ishmael.

> *"We cannot do the will of God until
> we have the grace of God to do it."* v.9

17. God's covenant of circumcision instituted.

18. Abraham intercedes for Sodom.

19. Lot delivered out of Sodom.

> *"Lot's wife became salt because her husband
> refused to be the salt of the earth."* v.26

> *"Lot became his own son's grandfather
> - what a shame!"* v. 37-38

20. Abraham deceives Abimelech concerning Sarah.

21. Birth of Isaac; rejection of Hagar and Ishmael.

> *"The well of salvation's waters cannot be seen
> until God opens our eyes."* v.19

22. Abraham offers up Isaac.

23. Sarah dies; Abraham buys burial plot.

24. Abraham seeks a wife for Isaac – Rebekeh.

> *"Even well-meaning Christians will try to delay you
> from instant obedience."* v.55

> *"When you know what is right to do, do it."* v.58

25. Abraham remarries; He dies; Ishmael dies; Jacob and Esau.

26. Isaac deceives men of Gerar about his wife; Isaac digs wells.

27. Jacob gains the blessing from his father by deception.

28. Jacob leaves home; His vow at Bethel.

29. Jacob works for Laban. He is deceived concerning Rachel and Leah.

30. Jacob's children; God increases Jacob's flock.

> *"In Bible days, women counted it a privilege
> to bear children."* v. 23

31. Jacob leaves for home; He is protected from Laban.

32. Jacob prepares to meet Esau; He wrestles with angel.

33. Jacob and Esau reunited.

34. Dinah is defiled; Brothers slay men of Shechem.

> *"Trouble comes when you want the benefits of marriage
> without the bond of marriage."* v. 3-7

35. Jacob returns to Bethel; Rachel dies in birthing Benjamin; Isaac dies.

> *"No one sins alone or in secret."* v. 22

36. Descendants of Esau.

37. Joseph's dreams; Joseph sold by his brothers into Egypt.

> *"Sin that is tolerated is sin that will control you."*
> - Daniel Knickerbocker v. 4-20

38. Judah and Tamar.

39. Joseph in Potipher's house; Joseph in prison.

40. Joseph tells dreams and fulfillment for Butler and Baker.

> *"Joseph could be glad and not sad,
> because he had done nothing bad."* v. 1-7

*"You may be forgotten by friends,
but you are not forsaken by God."* v. 23

41. Joseph tells Pharaoh's two dreams; Joseph promoted.

"There is a fault in forgetting the faithful." v. 9

42. Joseph meets his brothers who come to Egypt for food.

"God's providence is never coincidence." v. 46-57

43. Joseph sees brothers second time with Benjamin; Feeds them.

44. Joseph charges brothers with theft of cup; Judah pleads for Benjamin.

"Instead of shifting the blame, shoulder the blame." v. 32

45. Joseph reveals himself; makes provision in Egypt for father and family.

*"Joseph said, 'You sold me, but God sent me.'
Joseph saved the lives of those who wanted to take his."* v. 5-7

46. Jacob and family move to Egypt in Goshen.

47. Jacob blesses Pharaoh; Joseph feeds the people.

48. Jacob blesses Ephraim and Manasseh, and Joseph.

49. Jacob blesses and prophesies concerning his twelve sons.

50. Joseph buries Jacob; Joseph dies.

"Forgiveness allows us to be far-sighted." v. 20

EXODUS

1. Pharaoh enslaves the Hebrews.

2. Moses delivered by Pharaoh's daughter; Moses flees to Midian.

3. Moses meets God at the burning bush.

4. God's signs to Moses; Moses' excuses; Moses and Aaron go to Egypt.

> *"God will often bless and multiply the very thing*
> *we deem unimportant (a rod)."* v. 2-4

5. Pharaoh increases tasks of the Hebrew slaves.

6. God's covenant to Moses; the genealogy of Moses.

7. Plague #1 – River turned to blood.

8. Plague #2 – Frogs;
   Plague #3 – Lice;
   Plague #4 – Flies.

> *"If you want God to hear your voice,*
> *you had better hear His voice.* v. 12-13

9. Plague #5 – Cattle die;
   Plague #6 – Boils;
   Plague #7 – Thunder, hail.

10. Plague #8 – Locusts;
    Plague #9 – Darkness.

> *"God often raises up the wicked*
> *to show His power and get the glory."* v.16

11. Warning of final plague.

12. Plague #10 – Death of firstborn; Passover is instituted.

13. Israel leaves Egypt; reminded to keep Passover; Pillars of cloud and fire.

14. Israel crosses the Red Sea.

15. Song of Moses; Waters healed; the people murmur about bitter water.

> *"The cross turns a bitter life into sweetness."* v. 25

16. Murmured about lack of food; God gives manna and quail.

17. Murmured about lack of water; Water from rock; Moses, Aaron, Hur lead Israel against Amalek.

18. Jethro's advice for Moses to share the load of leadership.

19. Moses called up to Mt. Sinai; People forbidden to touch the mountain.

*"God leads us not only to a place
but to a person - Himself."* v. 4

20. The Ten Commandments

21. Laws concerning servants, killing, kidnapping, cursing, animals.

22. Restitution for theft, various trespasses.

23. Various laws: moral and religious; Sabbaths, feasts, and first fruits.

24. Moses is in the Mount for 40 days.

*"Are you a thermometer that adjusts to the temperature or a thermostat
that dictates the atmosphere?"* v. 12-18

25. Instructions for the Tabernacle: Ark of Covenant, Table of Shewbread, Candlestick.

26. Curtains of Tabernacle, with bars, taches, loops, boards, sockets, veil.

27. Brazen altar, court, gate of the court, olive oil.

28. Garments of the priests: breastplate, girdles, bonnets, breaches.

29. Consecrating the priests with blood and oil; Continual offerings.

30. Altar of Incense, atonement money, brass laver, holy oil.

31. Bezallel and Aholiab given wisdom to build Tabernacle and furniture.

32. The Golden Calf.

> *"The day the people put the pressure on the preacher."* v. 1-2

33. God withdraws His presence, but reveals Himself to Moses.

34. The Law rewritten, laws reviewed, Moses' face shines.

> *"Others notice when you have been with God,*
> *though you may not see what others see.*
> *(Moses' face shown, though Moses was not aware of it)"* v. 29

35. Offering received from the people for materials of Tabernacle.

36. Making and constructing the Tabernacle.

37. Making Ark of Covenant, Table of Shewbread, Candlestick, Altar of Incense, and Oil.

38. Making the Brazen Altar, Laver.

39. The Holy garments, breastplate, robe, linen coats.

40. Erection of Tabernacle, placing of the furniture; God's glory filled the place.

LEVITICUS

1. The Burnt Offering of the herd, the flock or fowl.

2. The Meat Offering of flour, oil and salt, frankincense.

3. The Peace Offering of the herd or the flock.

4. The Sin Offering for individual, whole congregation, or ruler.

5. The Trespass Offering of the flock or fowl.

6. Priestly procedures for each offering listed above.

7. Priestly procedures for each above offering continued.

8. Moses consecrates Aaron and his sons before the congregation at the Tabernacle.

9. Aaron's first offerings (Burnt, Sin, Peace, Meat Offerings).

10. Nadab and Abihu are killed for offering strange fire. Rules for eating offerings.

11. Clean and unclean foods.

12. Sacrifice for newborns.

13. Procedure for determining leprosy.

14. Procedure for cleansing the leper.

15. Laws of cleansing men and women who have an issue of blood/body fluids.

16. The Scapegoat offering in the Holy of Holies.

17. Injunction to offer sacrifice for sin only at the Tabernacle.

18. Sexual prohibitions.

19. Laws governing religious, moral, relationship behavior.

20. Laws governing religious and sexual behavior (occult, homosexuality, bestiality).

21. Standards for the priests.

22. Rules regarding holy things.

23. Feasts – Passover, First fruits, Trumpets, Day of Atonement, Tabernacles.

24. Making showbread; Punishing a blasphemer.

*"An attack on God's name is an attack on God.
You will not get away with it.* v.15-16

*"If you love God you will use His name only in prayer, praise,
personal witness or preaching, but never in vain."*

25. Law of inheritance and possession of land.

26. Exhortation and Warning: penalties for sin; mercy for the righteous.

27. Law of paying vows and tithes.

NUMBERS

1. Moses numbers the people after leaving Egypt.

2. Location of tribes around the Tabernacle; Order of movement.

3. Descendants of Levi and their service.

4. Duties of Kohathites, Gershonites, sons of Merari; age limit.

5. Separation of lepers; Offerings are the priests'; Trial by water for jealousy.

6. Law of the Nazarite; Priest's blessing.

7. Offerings of the princes of each tribe.

8. Purification and service of the Levites.

9. Exceptions to keeping Passover; Cloud on the Tabernacle.

10. Blowing trumpet alarms; Order of the march from Sinai to Paran.

11. Complainers burned; mixed multitude lusts for bread; 70 chosen leaders.

12. Miriam struck with leprosy for complaining about Moses' wife.

13. Twelve spies sent into Canaan.

14. People murmur concerning giants; Moses intercedes; Amalek defeats Israel.

> *"Fighting in the Flesh will Fail."* v.42-45

15. Laws concerning offerings; Sabbath-breaker stoned.

16. Korah's rebellion and demise.

> *"Be content to be what God has chosen you to be."* v. 9
> *"You must be broken before God will build you."* v.1-11
> *"Opportunities include Obligations."* v.1-11
> *"Carnal Christians cannot discern God's character and hand of discipline."* v. 41

17. Aaron's rod buds and produces almonds.

18. Levites get the tithe for their inheritance.

19. Ashes of a red heifer for purification of Israel.

20. Moses smites the rock twice; Miriam's death; Aaron's death.

21. Israel defeats Canaanites; Complain of no bread; Serpents bite; Sihon and Og defeated.

22. Balaam and his talking ass.

> *"A Christian in disobedience is blind to God's presence (Balaam)."* v. 31

23. Balaam blesses Israel against his will.

> *"What you say is more important than where you say it."* v. 27

24. Balaam prophesies of Israel's coming conquests.

25. Israel commits whoredom with Moabites; Guilty are executed and plagued.

26. Moses numbers the people for war.

27. The daughters of Zelophehad; Joshua chosen for leadership.

28. Laws for offerings on special days.

29. Laws for offerings on special days.

30. Law of the vow for men and women.

31. Israel smites the Midianites; Dividing the booty (spoil).

32. God grants Reuben and Gad's request for their inheritance to be east of Jordan.

33. Journeys of Israel in wilderness chronicled.

34. Borders of the inheritance.

35. Cities of Refuge.

36. Heiresses must marry within their tribe.

DEUTERONOMY

1. Moses reviews the trip from Egypt to Canaan; Twelve spies; Forty years in wilderness.

2. Israel passes through land of Esau, Moab, Ammon; Fight with Amorites (Sihon).

3. Israel defeats Og of Bashan; God chooses Joshua to lead the people.

4. Moses reminds the people to keep God's law; Appoints Cities of Refuge.

5. Restatement of the Ten Commandments.

6. Reminder for parents to teach their children the Commandments.

7. Reject the gods of the heathen; None of their diseases; God will drive them out.

*"God gives dynamic deliverances to build
confidence for future victories."* v.15

8. Remember the Lord Who will give you the land and wealth.

9. Israel told to be humble; Moses rehearses their past rebellions.

10. Recounting how the Tables of Stone were restored; Love God and fellowman.

11. Remembering God's miracles; Remember and keep God's Commandments.

12. Don't forget to sacrifice and tithe; Don't eat blood.

13. Discerning false prophets; How to test them; They are to be destroyed.

14. Peculiar people in appearance, in diet, in tithing.

15. The seventh year: release from debt; bond slaves.

16. Keeping the feasts: Passover, Feast of Weeks, of Tabernacles; Judges.

17. Idolaters to be executed; Process of judging cases; Guidelines for kings.

18. The Levite's provision; Reject abominations of the heathen; A future Prophet is promised.

19. Cities of Refuge.

20. Fear not the enemy; Exceptions to military service; Wartime laws.

21. Rid of innocent blood; Captive women; Stubborn sons.

22. Proper treatment of neighbor's property; Laws concerning chastity.

23. Those prohibited from the Sanctuary; Handling personal cleanliness; Vows.

24. Divorce and remarriage; Justice on many topics.

25. Punishment; Taking a brother's widow; False weights.

26. Remembering God's deliverance; Tithes.

27. Law to be written on stones; Cursings and Blessings.

28. Blessings and Cursings.

29. Moses exhorts the people to obey; God's wrath against disobedience.

> *"Don't worry about the unrevealed;*
> *live up to that which is revealed."* v. 29

30. God gives choices of blessing and cursing.

31. Moses encourages Joshua and the people.

> *"The fear of God must both be taught and caught."* v. 12

32. The Song of Moses.

33. Moses blesses the tribes.

34. Moses dies.

JOSHUA

1. God instructs Joshua to be strong and courageous.

2. Two men spy out Jericho.

3. The people pass over Jordan on dry ground.

4. Joshua builds a memorial of twelve stones.

5. Gilgal – the place where the new generation was circumcised.

6. Jericho defeated – walls come down; Rahab and family spared.

> *"God's plan for victory is always*
> *geared to bring Him the glory."* v. 5

7. Defeat at Ai; Discovery of Achan's sin and his execution.

> *"Sin will take away your spiritual power;*
> *it is the roadblock to success."* v. 1-6

8. Destruction of Ai; Joshua reads the Law of Moses to the people.

9. Joshua deceived by crafty Gibeonites; Gibeonites become servants.

> *"Prayerlessness will cause us to lack discernment."* v. 1-14
>
> *"Vows are meant to be kept."* v. 20

10. Joshua destroys five kings, Delivers Gibeonites; God sends hail; Sun stands still.

> *"You cannot hide from God; Your hiding place*
> *may one day be your grave."* v. 27

11. Ten armies destroyed by Joshua.

12. List of 31 kings defeated by Joshua.

13. Canaan divided among the tribes.

14. Caleb requests and conquers Hebron.

15. Territory and cities of Judah; Caleb's daughter asks for a blessing of springs.

16. Territory of Ephraim.

17. Territory of Manasseh; Promise to destroy Canaanites.

18. Territory of Benjamin.

19. Territories of Simeon, Zebulon, Issachar, Asher, Naphtali, Dan.

20. Six Cities of Refuge appointed.

21. Cities given to the Levites by the other tribes.

22. Two and one-half tribes return to inheritance east of Jordan; They build an altar "Ed."

23. Joshua's farewell address: Depend on God, obey the Lord for blessing.

24. Joshua speaks to leaders; Joshua dies; Joseph buried; Eliezar dies.

JUDGES

1. Judah and Simeon fight together to take their possessions (inheritance).

2. Israel rebuked for making leagues with Canaanites; Another generation.

   "God sometimes allows the enemy to prevail to test us." 2:21-22

3. Nations left to test their physical and spiritual strength; Othniel, Ehud, Shamgar. Ehud kills Eglon - "The day lefty let fatty have it."

4. Deborah, Barak and Jael defeat Sisera, Jabin's captain.

   "Recognizing the seriousness of our sin is the key to ridding ourselves of it and being restored." Brad Phillips v. 3

5. Deborah's victory song.

6. Gideon's call; Destruction of Baal's idol; Tests of the fleece.

   "God uses unlikely people to do impossible things to get unusual results." v. 16

7. Gideon separates the fearful and foolish from his army; victory with 300.

8. Ephraim complains; Zebah & Zalmunna defeated; His ephod; Gideon dies.

   "It is not when you started, but how you finish." v. 1-3

9. Abimelech kills his 70 brethren; Abimelech dies, result of Jotham's curse.

10. Judges Tola and Jair; Israel captive to Ammonites; They repent.

11. Jephthah chosen to lead; His message to Ammon; His vow and victory.

12. Jephthah defeats Ephraim; "Shibboleth"; Judges Elon and Abdon.

13. Angelic announcement concerning birth of Samson.

14. Samson's riddle and payment.

15. Uses 300 foxes to burn crops; Kills 1,000 with jawbone; Drinks from jawbone.

16. Samson carries city gates; Delilah traps him; Samson dies with Philistines.

17. Micah hires a Levite to be his personal priest.

18. The Danites take Micah's Levite; They dwell in Laish (Dan).

19. A Levite's concubine is abused by Gibeonites; She is divided and sent throughout Israel.

20. Israel fights Benjamites who defended Gibeonites; Victory with an ambush.

21. Wives provided for Benjamites from Jabesh-Gilead and Shiloh.

RUTH

1. Naomi leaves Bethlehem for Moab; Returns with daughter-in-law Ruth. (Love's Resolve) (Death)

   "Love will make you cleave, when others want to leave." v. 14

2. Ruth finds grace in eyes of Boaz; She gleans only in his fields. (Love's Response) (Dedication)

   "The gleanings of the Christian are better than the vintage of the unsaved."

3. Naomi makes her inheritance available (including Ruth) to Boaz. (Love's Request) (Direction)

4. Boaz purchases the inheritance and marries Ruth; Line of David (Christ) (Love's Reward) (Delight)

I SAMUEL

1. Samuel is born and lent to the Lord in answer to Hannah's prayer.

   "Hannah was a bride that was barren, burdened, begging, believing, bearing, bringing and blessed." Dan Knickerbocker

2. Hannah's song of praise; Eli's wicked sons; God rebukes Eli.

3. God calls Samuel, confirms his judgment on house of Eli.

   "Eli did not watch out for his church, his family, or his belly."

4. Eli's sons slain in battle with Philistines; Eli dies; Ichabod is born.

   "The presence of God is a blessing to the believer (Ebenezer), but a curse to the un-believer (Icabod)." v. 21

5. Philistines capture Ark and suffer emerods as a result.

6. Philistines return Ark on cart with two milk cows; Israel men killed for looking in the Ark of the Covenant.

7. God thundered against the Philistines for a victory ("Ebenezer").

8. The people ask for a king; God warns them of the cost.

9. Saul seeks his father's asses; Dines with Samuel; Is told of being chosen king.

   "Those in the wrong, desire compassion for themselves; but those in the right desire direction from God." v. 9-21

10. Saul is anointed and proclaimed first king of Israel.

11. Saul delivers Jabesh-Gilead from the Ammonites.

12. Samuel is honored; Warns the people about wanting a king; It thunders and rains.

13. Saul's hasty sacrifice; God rejects Saul.

14. Jonathan's and armor-bearer's victory; Philistines flee; Saul's foolish fast; Saul threatens Jonathan.

15. Saul's disobedience in sparing the best when told to slay Amalek.

   "Good is always the enemy of best." - Walter McDaniel v. 13-23

16. Samuel anoints David; David plays harp for Saul.

   "First best - having the Spirit v. 13;

   Second best - being with one who has the Spirit v. 18;

   Third best - the Spirit using you against your will 19:23"

17. David kills Goliath; Saul envies David.

18. David and Jonathan's friendship; Saul's attempt to destroy David with dowry.

   "Criticism: listen to it, learn from it, love through it, live through it."
   - Shane Skelton v. 9-15

   "Jealousy, suspicion and fear creates enemies." v. 28-29

19. Saul's attempts to kill David with javelin; Delivered by Jonathan and Michal.

20. Jonathan and David's covenant; Jonathan uses three arrows to warn David.

21. David eats the showbread; David before King Achish acts the madman.

22. David and his 400 men; Doeg slays 85 priests at Saul's decree.

23. David delivers city of Keilah; flees with 600 men; Pursued by Saul.

24. David spares Saul in the cave; cuts off skirt of his robe; Saul repents.

25. Samuel dies; David takes Abigail after God kills Nabal.

26. David again spares Saul; Takes his spear and cruse; Saul again repents.

*"David always appealed to the spiritual side of Saul,
which held him in check - called him the 'Lord's anointed'."*

27. David escapes to Gath; Is given Ziklag; Wars against Amalek; Deceives king.

28. Saul seeks witch's advice; Samuel announces his demise.

29. David is spared having to fight with Philistines against Saul.

30. Ziklag is burned by Amalekites; He encourages himself; Recovers all.

"You may give up just before your greatest blessings come." v. 4-6

"If you attempt the possible, God will do the impossible." v. 18

31. Saul dies in battle; is buried by the men of Jabesh-Gilead.

II SAMUEL

1. David executes Amalekite who claimed to have killed Saul; David laments the deaths of Saul and Jonathan.

"David and Jonathan had a love that passes the love of women; whereas, homosexuals have a love that replaces the love of women." v. 26

2. David made king over Judah; Civil war; Abner kills Asahel.

3. Abner brings Israel to David; Joab kills Abner; David mourns Abner.

4. Two captains kill Ishbosheth; David executes them.

5. David anointed king of Israel; David's children; he twice defeats Philistines.

"Wait for God before Going." v. 24

6. David brings Ark on new cart; Uzzah killed; Michal rebukes David's dancing.

7. David's desire to build God a house, David's prayer and praise.

8. David defeats his enemies; His government cabinet.

9. The fetching of Mephibosheth.

10. Hanun, Ammon king, shames David's servants; David defeats Ammon and Syria.

11. David defeats the Ammonites and Syrians; David, Bathsheba and Uriah.

"Uriah had more character while drunk, than David had while sober."
(illustration of back-slidden believers) v. 1-13

12. Nathan exposes David's sin; David and Bathsheba's child dies.

"Fear of the Lord - When God's frown is our greatest dread
and His smile is our greatest delight." v. 13

13. Amnon forces Tamar; Absalom kills Amnon.

14. Joab sends woman to king David to plead for Absalom; Absalom returns.

15. Absalom wins people's hearts; David flees Jerusalem; Zadok and Hushai to spy for David.

16. Ziba's lie; Shimei's cursing; Absalom goes in unto David's concubines.

17. The counsel of Ahithophel and Hushai; Barzillai brings food and bedding.

18. Absalom is killed; Ahimaaz and Cushi bring David the news; David weeps.

"A good reputation precedes a welcomed message." v. 27

19. King David returns; Speaks to Judah, Shimei, Mephibosheth and Barzillai.

20. Sheba rebels and is killed; Joab kills Amasa.

21. Gibeonites avenged by killing seven sons of Saul; Goliath's four sons killed.

22. David's Song of Deliverance. (see Psalm 18)

23. David's last words; David's mighty men.

24. David foolishly numbers people; God gives pestilence; David sacrifices.

I KINGS

1. Abishag warns the king; Adonijah rebels; Solomon is made king.

2. David instructs Solomon concerning Barzillai; Joab, Shimei, Adonijah are executed.

3. Solomon asks for wisdom; Judges between two harlots and their babies.

4. Solomon's officers; his daily provision; his wealth and wisdom.

5. Solomon's and Hiram's men hew lumber and stones for new Temple.

6. The gold and carvings of the completed Temple (magnificent).

7. Solomon's house and buildings; Temple pillars, molten sea on oxen, furniture.

8. Ark in the Temple; God's glory fills Temple; Solomon's prayer of dedication.

"In the Old Testament God has a Temple for His people;
in the New Testament God has a people for his Temple." v.11

9. God's conditional covenant; Solomon's gift cities to Hiram; His offerings three times a year.

10. Queen of Sheba visits Solomon; Solomon's gold, shields, throne, horses.

11. Solomon's wives and apostasy; Adversaries Hadad, Rezon, Jeroboam; Solomon dies.

12. Rehoboam's bad political decision on taxes; Jeroboam's bad religious decision (two idolatrous calves).

13. Man of God whither's Jeroboam's Hand; Believes lie of older prophet; is killed by lion.

14. Jeroboam's child dies at word of Abijah; Shishak plunders Jerusalem; Rehoboam dies.

15. Judah's kings – Abijam, Asa; Israel's kings – Nadab, Baasha.

16. Israel's kings – Elah, Zimri, Omri, Ahab; Hiel rebuilds Jericho, sons die.

17. Elijah and widow of Zarephath; Elijah raises her son from the dead.

18. Elijah's contest with Ahab on Mt. Carmel; Slays prophets of Baal.
    "Those who reject truth will believe a lie." v. 8
    "False gods mock their worshipers by not answering." v. 27

19. Elijah flees Jezebel; God speaks to him in the cave; Elisha chosen.

20. Ahab defeats Benhadad of Syria twice; Ahab rebuked for joining Benhadad.

21. Ahab takes Naboth's vineyard and is denounced by Elijah.

22. Ahab and Jehoshaphat battle Ramath-Gilead; Micaiah prophesies Ahab's death; Ahab dies.
    "We live in a day when "good" is wrong and "evil" is truth." v. 8
    "True gospel preachers are preachers of truth and peace." v. 17
    "God knows where to drop the arrow" - Tom Schulte v. 34

II KINGS

1. Elijah tells Ahaziah he will die; Elijah calls down fire on 100 of his soldiers.

2. Elijah is raptured in a chariot of fire; Bears attack children who mock Elisha.

   "When God removes His man and gives a replacement,
   don't seek the old leader, follow the new." v. 11-18

3. God defeats Moab for Jehoshaphat with ditches of water they think is blood.

4. Woman pays debt with oil; Elisha raises the Shunammite son; Death in the pot.

5. Naaman is healed of leprosy; Gehazi contracts the leprosy.

6. The axe head swims; Syrians blinded, led and released at Samaria – Famine.

   "The secret of prayer is prayer in secret." - Ravenhill v. 12

7. Four lepers announce God's deliverance from the Syrians.

   "Don't keep the good news to yourself." v. 9

   *"Preaching is one beggar telling another beggar
   where to find the Bread of Life."* v.8-11

8. Hazael suffocates Benhadad; Joram of Judah marries Ahab's daughter Athaliah.

9. Jehu is anointed king; Slays kings Joram and Ahaziah and Queen Jezebel.

10. Jehu slays 70 sons of Ahab; Slays priests and worshipers of Baal.

11. Athaliah slays seed royal; Joash is hidden; Later made king; Athaliah killed.

12. Jehoash repairs the Temple; Pays Hazael of Syria to leave him alone.

13. Jehu's son Jehoahaz did evil; Oppressed by Syria; Delivered by son Joash; Elisha dies.

14. Amaziah meddles with Judah; Jerusalem is plundered; Amaziah killed by conspiracy.

15. Uzziah dies a leper; Shallum slays Zachariah; Menahem slays Shallum; Pekah slays Pekahiah; Hoshea slays Pekah.

16. Ahaz defeats Syria; adopts altar of Damascus.

17. Assyrian captivity of Israel because of idolatry; Samaritans "fear God" and serve other gods.

18. Hezekiah's reign and revival; Jerusalem threatened by Assyrians; Rabshakeh threatens.

19. Isaiah prophesies Rabshakeh's demise; Angel slays 185,000; Sennacherib killed by sons.

20. Hezekiah recovers of boil, given 15 years; Sun dial goes back; Hezekiah dies, Manasseh becomes king.

21. Manasseh seduces Judah into idolatry; Wicked Amon killed by servants.

22. Josiah's reform; Repairs the Temple; The Law is found, read and obeyed.

23. Josiah's reforms continue; Burned Baal vessels; Kept Passover; Slain by Pharaoh.

24. Nebuchadnezzar invades, removes kings; Appoints Zedekiah who rebels.

25. Nebuchadnezzar conquers and destroys Jerusalem; He carries Judah into captivity.

I CHRONICLES

1. Sons of Japheth, Ham, Shem, Abraham, Esau, Kings and dukes of Edom.

2. Sons of Israel, Judah, Jesse, Hezron, Jerahmeel, Caleb, Kenites.

3. Sons of David; Line of Solomon, sons of Jeconiah.

4. Line of Judah; Prayer of Jabez; Line of Chelub; Sons of Shelah; Simeon.

5. Line of Reuben, Gad, half of Manasseh; Carried captive by Assyrians for idolatry.

6. Line of Levi; Eleazar, Gershom, Merari, Kohath, their dwellings.

7. Line of Issachar; Benjamin, Naphtali, Manasseh, Ephraim, Asher.

8. Line of Benjamin; Saul.

9. Dwellers in Jerusalem: priests, porters, Levites, singers; Line of Saul.

10. An account of the death of Saul and reason for it.

11. David made king; List and exploits of his mighty men.

12. Those who followed David while running from Saul, in Ziklag and in Hebron.

13. David transports the Ark on a new cart; Uzza touches it and is killed.

14. David's many wives and children; He defeats Philistines twice.

15. David brings the Ark to Jerusalem in the right manner.

16. David sacrifices; His song; Appoints priests and musicians.

17. Nathan tells David that Solomon will build God's house instead of him.

18. God preserves David in war; Dedicates the silver and gold plundered; His political cabinet.

19. David's messengers to Hanun are shamed; David defeats Ammon and Syria.

20. David destroys and plunders Ammonites; David's men kill the giants.

21. David sins in numbering Israel; Pays with pestilence; He sacrifices.

    "A sacrifice which costs you nothing is no sacrifice at all." v. 24

22. David prepares materials for the Temple; Instructs Solomon and princes.

23. David assigns the duties of the priests and Levites.

24. Duties of the Sons of Aaron, over the House of God.

25. Divisions and duties of the singers and musicians.

26. Divisions of the porters (strong men), and Levites over the treasury.

27. The captains for each month; his officers.

28. David gives Solomon final instructions about building the Temple.

29. People give willingly for the Temple; David's prayer; His death; Solomon king.

II CHRONICLES

1. Solomon asks for wisdom; He multiplies chariots, horses, gold and silver.

2. Solomon asks Hiram for skilled workers and cedar; Uses strangers as laborers.

3. Description of the new Temple; Gold, cherubims, veils, pillars.

4. Furnishings of Temple; Molten sea, lavers, candlesticks, snuffers, basins, spoons.

5. Ark brought into the Temple; Music; God's glory fills the House.

6. Solomon's prayer of dedication.

7. God's glory fills the Temple; 142,000 animals sacrificed; God warns the people.

8. Solomon's building projects and organization; Gold he obtained.

9. Queen of Sheba's visit and gifts; Solomon's throne; His wealth; His death.

10. Rehoboam takes unwise advice; Nation divides; Jeroboam gets Israel; Rehoboam gets Judah.

11. Rehoboam's building projects; His wives and children; Jeroboam's idolatry.

12. Shishak of Egypt plunders but preserves Jerusalem before Rehoboam forsakes God.

13. Abijah's speech to Jeroboam; God delivers Judah; Abijah's family.

14. Asa's reforms and city building; Defeats Zerah the Ethiopian and spoils them.

15. Prophet Azariah encourages Asa; Revival resulting in peace.

16. Asa hires Syrians against Israel; Is rebuked by Hanani the seer; Dies diseased.

17. Jehoshaphat removed false worship, taught the people; His mighty men.

18. Jehoshaphat goes with Ahab against Syria; Ahab is killed.

19. Jehoshaphat appoints judges and Levites and charges them.

20. Ammon, Moab, Edom defeated by Levites singing and praising God.

21. Jehoram is resisted by surrounding nations; Dies with diseased bowels.

22. Ahaziah, slain by Jehu; Athaliah kills king's sons except Joash; She reigns.

23. Joash made king; Athaliah is slain.

24. Joash repairs Temple; After Jehoiadah dies Joash apostatizes; Is diseased and dies by conspiracy.

25. Amaziah defeats Edom; Serves their gods; Defeated by Syria; Dies by conspiracy.

26. Good King Uzziah: builder, husbandman; Wrongfully sacrificed, Died with leprosy.

"Pride in prayer causes power to perish." v. 16

27. Good King Jotham built much; Fought Ammon, put under tribute; Ended well.

28. Ahaz serves Baal; Is defeated by Syria; Israel worships enemies' gods.

29. Hezekiah repairs the Temple and restores the worship of God.

30. Hezekiah and all Judah keep the Passover and rejoice.

31. People destroy their idols; Bring the tithe; Provision for priests and Levites.

32. Hezekiah resists Sennacherib; Angel kills Assyrians; Hezekiah healed.

33. Manasseh's idolatry, affliction, repentance, restoration; Amon's idolatry; Conspiracy by Amon's servants.

34. Josiah repairs Temple, reads Law; Institutes reforms.

35. Josiah keeps Passover; Is killed while meddling in Egypt's war.

"Don't fight battles that are not yours to fight." v. 21

36. Reigns of Jehoahaz, Jehoiakim, Jehoiachin, Zedekiah; 70-year captivity; Cyrus allows return.

"When God's compassion is ignored, He will turn us over to those with no compassion." v. 15-17

EZRA

1. Cyrus, king of Persia, sanctions rebuilding of Jerusalem Temple.

2. People who returned from captivity 42,360 plus 7,337 servants.

3. Sacrifice and worship restored; Foundation of Temple is laid.

4. Work ceases because of adversaries' lawsuit to Artaxerxes.

"Frustration is the gap between our expectations and our experience." v. 1-6

5. Prophets encourage work on Temple and wall; Enemies report to Darius.

6. Darius validates the decree of Cyrus; Jews complete building; Keep Passover.

7. Ezra arrives to teach the Law; He is helped financially by the king.

8. List of those who returned with Ezra; Prayed for protection; Arrived in Jerusalem safely.

"Faith furthers the work of God and blesses the people of God." v. 36

9. Jews had married the heathen; Ezra mourns and prays for mercy.

10. A list of men who vowed to put away their strange wives.

NEHEMIAH

1. Nehemiah learns of the condition of Jerusalem and prays to God for deliverance.

2. Nehemiah gets permission to build walls of Jerusalem; Views the walls; Rejects Sanballat's help.

3. The people are organized, and the wall is repaired.

4. Sanballat and Tobiah mock the work, threaten to attack; Nehemiah prepares their defense.

5. Nehemiah abolishes the usury charged among the Jews to each other.

6. Sanballat plots to stop the building with meetings and false accusations.

7. Genealogy and list of those who returned to Jerusalem from Babylon.

8. Ezra reads the Law; People mourn over sin; Rejoice in cleansing; Feast of Tabernacles.

   "Preaching is reading, explaining and illustrating." v. 8

9. Ezra reminds the people of their good and bad history; God's graciousness.

10. A covenant is sealed to keep the Law, to correct marriages, to tithe.

11. People at Jerusalem: of Judah, Benjamin, Levites (singers).

12. List of Levites; Dedication of the wall; Musicians; Rejoicing; Giving.

13. Tobiah thrown out of Temple; Priests receive provision and Sabbath is restored; Foreign wives are removed.

ESTHER

1. Queen Vashti is demoted for disobedience to King Ahasuerus.

2. Esther is chosen Queen; Mordecai prevents an assassination of the king.

3. Haman passes law to destroy all Jews for his hatred of Mordecai.

4. Esther fasts for three days before going to the King.

5. Esther invites the king and Haman to first banquet; Haman builds gallows for Mordecai.

6. The king honors Mordecai by having Haman lead his horse; Haman is shamed.

7. Esther exposes Haman at the second banquet; Haman is hanged on his own gallows.

8. Mordecai writes a new law for Jews to defend themselves; Disaster to delight.

"Our sin nature has not been removed;
God gave us a new one so now we can choose." v. 7-14

9. Jews defend themselves; Feast of Purim established.

10. The acts and greatness of the King and Mordecai.

JOB

1. Job's good life; Satan's challenge; Job loses his wealth.

"God proved Job, He didn't judge him."

2. Job loses his health; His friends come to mourn.

3. Job wishes he had never been born; Extols the virtues of death.

4. Eliphaz – You faint in trouble; His dream; Shall man be more just than God?

5. Eliphaz (continued) – Sin tends to ruin; Despise not God's chastening.

6. Job – My sorrow cannot be measured; You dig a pit for your friend – me.

7. Job – My life is wind; Why do you scare me with dreams?

8. Bildad – Do you charge God with wrong? The hypocrite's hope shall perish.

9. Job – How can man be just with God? He destroys both the perfect and the wicked; I need a Daysman.

10. Job – Complains that God is judging a righteous man.

11. Zophar – Defends God's treatment of Job; "Job, confess and find mercy!"

12. Job – Takes offense at their spirit; I know God did this and how He works.

13. Job – I will trust in God, though He slay me, but you speak falsely for God.

14. Job – The transient nature of man: dies and does not revive like a tree.

15. Eliphaz – How can you justify yourself before God? The wicked have trouble and anguish.

16. Job – Denounces his merciless friends; cries out for intercessor with God.

17. Job – I am rejected and made a byword; unwise friends; No hope but a grave.

18. Bildad – Job rebukes us, yet it is the wicked that fall into snares and know not God.

19. Job – God destroys me; family and friends forsake me; I know that my Redeemer liveth.

20. Zophar – The wicked hide their sin, but it is soon revealed and judged by God.

21. Job – Why do many wicked prosper? Many never pay for sin till they die.

22. Eliphaz – If you would repent of sin, God would forgive, bless and deliver you.

23. Job – I want to plead with God; He has tried me as gold; made my heart soft.

"When Job could not find God, God found him." v. 8-10

24. Job – The heartless sins of the wicked; Their destruction.

25. Bildad – How can a man be justified before God? Man is a worm.

26. Job – How have you helped with counsel? God's power is seen in creation.

27. Job – I maintain my righteous ways; The losses of the wicked.

28. Job – Where can wisdom be found? In the fear of God and refusing evil.

29. Job – Job recounts his former respect, influence and service to others.

30. Job – Is mocked by worthless men; Though I've helped others, I'm rejected.

31. Job – If I have done wrong, then let wrong come on me; he justifies himself.

32. Elihu – Must speak; Job, you justify yourself; Friends, you have no answers.

33. Elihu – We cannot question God; God will reward the righteous.

34. Elihu – You cannot charge God foolishly; God is no respecter of persons.

35. Elihu – God is not personally affected by your goodness or sin; Trust in God.

36. Elihu – How God works with kings; God's wisdom cannot be known.

37. Elihu – God does things we cannot comprehend.

38. God – God's wisdom in creation is a mystery to man.

39. God – More questions Job cannot answer: concerning the ass, unicorn, horse, ostrich, and eagle.

40. Job and God – Job confesses his sin; God continues with questions about His creation: dinosaurs.

41. God – What about leviathan?

42. Job and God – Job admits ignorance, repents; Friends rebuked; Job is blessed.

PSALMS

1. What the godly and ungodly men are like.

2. God laughs at the heathen and blesses the faithful.

3. God gives peace and safety in the presence of the enemy.

4. Trust in God turns distress into gladness.

5. Prayer and trust in God is the answer to dealing with the enemy.

6. Enemies cause fear and weeping in the night; Prayer will comfort me.

7. God is my defense against the enemy; He will validate me.

8. The wonder that God would take notice of man.

9. God, the righteous judge, will punish the nations that forget Him.

10. The proud lifestyle of the wicked; God is the Judge for the oppressed.

11. If the foundations be destroyed, what can the righteous do? He trieth the wicked.

12. Help, Lord, the proud prevail; God's word is purified and preserved forever.

Re: King James and other Bibles:
"If the king is not on it, the King is not in it." v.6,7

13. How long will God forget me while under attack? I will trust His salvation.

"Here we see David's plea, his prayer, and his praise."

14. The fool says there is no God; None good; When God saves, we rejoice.

15. God accepts all who are right in their walk, talk, look, money.

16. The joy of being in the presence of the Lord.

17. I will seek God's help when surrounded by oppressors.

"In God we are held up v. 5, heard v. 6, helped v. 7, and hid v. 8."

18. God is my deliverer, encourager, rewarder and Savior.

19. Creation declares God's glory; His Word is more precious than gold.

20. The king blesses the people; We will trust in God and not in armies.

21. The king trusts God to defend against His enemies.

22. Prophecy of Christ's death; Witness to the nations of this event.

"The Cross, the Savior; Yesterday, Provision"
(see Ch. 23-24 for rest of outline)

23. The shepherd leads, feeds, defends, and restores his flock.

"The Crook, the Shepherd, Today; Protection"

24. Only the righteous can approach the Creator, the King of Glory.

"The Crown; the Sovereign, Forever; Prospect"

25. Remember Thy mercies; Remember not my sins.

26. My foot will not slide because I walk in Thy truth.

27. I will wait on the Lord who is my salvation.

28. Keep me from dissemblers; God will destroy them; I will sing to Him.

29. The voice of the Lord is behind all His great works.

30. I extol thee for thy deliverance and protection.

31. Into thine hand I commit my spirit in the midst of those who reproach me.

32. David's confession of sin; God is my hiding place; Be not stubborn.

"To get your prayer answered,
you must get your prayer heard." Jerry Nye v. 5

33. Praise the Lord with music; Blessed the nation who trusts in the Lord.

34. Magnify the Lord; The angel of the Lord delivers His own; Fear the Lord.

35. Let the wicked be shamed and destroyed by the righteous; Their steps slide.

36. The wicked flatters himself; God's mercy is toward the righteous.

37. Thirty promises for the righteous; Their steps shall not slide.

38. I feel the effect of my sin; Forsake me not, make haste to help me.

39. The musings of a silent tongue; His hope is in God.

40. A song of testimony; Preaching to the congregation; Shame my persecutors.

41. Strengthen me in sickness; My friend betrays me; God upholds me.

42. My heart pants for God; My hope in God is the health of my countenance.

43. Hope in God in the midst of an ungodly nation; I will worship and trust.

44. Though the enemy oppose, we have not forgotten Thee; Save us!

45. The bride prepares herself for the King; She is described.

46. God is our refuge and strength; He will destroy the heathen.

47. Sing praises to the King who reigns over the earth.

48. God is glorified among the kings of the earth when they see Jerusalem.

49. The way of the wealthy; Their wealth remains here; Ours will last forever.

50. God is independent of His creatures; He will expose the wicked.

51. David's confession of his sin with Bathsheba.

> *"Once you know God, you can never be satisfied without Him."* v. 10-12

> *"When you come to God about sin you need a broken heart; when you come to God with praise you need a whole heart."* v. 17

52. The righteous will laugh at the boasting and destruction of the wicked.

53. The fool says, "There is no God"; There is none good, no, not one.

54. Save me; God is my helper; He will deliver me.

55. When my friends turn against me, I will cast my burden on the Lord.

56. When I cry unto God, He puts my tears in a bottle.

57. I cry to God in my calamities; My heart is fixed on Him, therefore I will sing.

58. A call on God to judge the wicked, so the righteous can see His vengeance.

59. The God of my mercy will defend me against my enemies.

60. God's banner of truth is to be displayed; How He handles a heathen.

61. I will trust in God who hears my vows; He prolongs the king's life.

62. God is my defense from those who lie in wait; God rewards according to our work.

63. I thirst to see God's power and glory; He will stop the liars.

"If you don't get what you want, be thankful
you don't get what you don't want."

64. God will make the verbal arrows of the wicked to fall upon themselves.

65. God hears and answers prayer; He meets the physical needs of the earth.

66. God proves men by His wonderful works; He has heard my prayer.

67. Let the people praise God; then God will bless us.

68. God is everything we need: to fatherless and widows, enemy, earth (rain).

69. My enemies mock me; judge them, Lord; I will trust your deliverance.

70. O God, make haste to help all those who love thy salvation.

71. Help me; my hope is in thee, even in my old age.

72. God shall be the judge; All the earth shall bow down before Him.

73. The wicked prosper; but God will have the final word.

74. God, show your power to the wicked, as you have demonstrated it in the past.

75. Promotion comes from the north; God will judge the wicked.

76. The wrath of men shall praise Him; the remainder He will restrain.

77. I remember my song in the night; I will remember God's works and wonders.

78. Share with the next generation the miracles of our past.

"Can God? God Can!" - Harold Sightler v. 19

79. God, pour vengeance on our enemies; Forgive us and preserve the prisoners.

80. O, Shepherd of Israel, turn us, deliver us, save us.

81. Israel ignored good; He gave them to their lusts; Open thy mouth, I will fill it.

82. Injunction to do justice to the poor and needy.

83. Cry to deliver Israel from nations who would destroy them.

84. The joy of going to the House of the Lord.

85. Mercy, truth, righteousness indicate God's blessings on us.

86. Hear my cry; I trust in Thee; Show me a token for good.

87. Glorious things of Zion are spoken by the man who was born there.

88. The psalmist feels excluded from the help of anyone.

"Are you forgetting to remember or remembering to forget?" v. 12

89. I will sing of God's mercies, faithfulness and deliverance.

90. Teach us to number our days; Establish the work of our hands.

"Live for something that will outlast you." v. 16

"When we come into this world we cry and everyone rejoices. When we come to die, we should have lived so that everyone else will cry while we rejoice." - Don Strange v. 9-17

91. The Soldier's psalm. The secret place is the place of refuge.

92. Praise God with music for His work; He will anoint me with fresh oil.

93. The Lord's majesty is demonstrated in the waves of the sea.

94. God will judge and revenge the wicked. He sees and hears all.

95. O come let us worship God; Hear his voice, harden not your heart.

96. Declare His glory among the heathen…all people…the nations.

97. The Lord is to be worshiped, even by the gods; He is exalted above all.

98. Sing and play instruments to the Lord for His perfect judgment.

99. A holy God deserves our worship; He answered the prophets of old.

100. Serve and praise the One who made us and gives us mercy and truth.

101. My house shall be a place of righteousness; entertaining good people

"Protect the eye-gate to your soul." v. 3

102. God hears the prayers of the destitute; Go to Him in time of need.

103. Bless God for His benefits, mercy, His kingdom, patience.

104. God created, controls and coordinates the forces of nature; Bless the Lord.

105. God's hand was behind all the events of Israel's history.

106. A history of Israel's constant rebellion, idolatry, judgment; His mercy restores.

"God may give you what you want,
but you may not want what you get." v. 15

107. God's deliverance to those who cry: the Redeemed, the Rebel, the Rogue, the Restless.

108. My heart is fixed to praise God for His mercy, truth and deliverance.

109. A plea for vengeance on the wicked; let his way come on his own head.

110. The Lord shall rule as a priest after the order of Melchizedek.

111. God speaks through His works; His name is revered.

112. A good man is righteous and discreet; His heart is fixed and established.

113. The Lord on high lifts up the lowly.

114. God's provision in the Wilderness.

115. Idols have no life or power; God is our help and shield.

116. God delivered my soul from death, mine eyes from tears, and my feet from falling.

117. Praise the Lord for His merciful kindness and truth.

118. Trust in the Lord; put no confidence in man or government.

119. Prayers, praises and professions of obedience to the Word of God.

"The more you are in the Word,
the less the World will be in you." v. 11

120. Deliver me from the deceitful, false tongue that desires war.

121. My help comes from the Keeper and Preserver of Israel.

122. Pray for the peace and prosperity of Jerusalem as you go to worship.

123. Our eyes wait upon the merciful God.

124. If God had not been on our side, we would be overwhelmed; We escaped.

125. The rod of the wicked will not rest on the righteous; God will do good to us.

126. God delivered from captivity; Sow in tears, reap in joy.

127. The Lord builds the house; Children are His heritage.

128. The blessed man is blessed in his family.

129. God will curse the enemies of Zion; they will be confounded.

130. There is forgiveness with God Who marks iniquities; I wait and hope in God.

131. I am humble and quiet before Thee; Our hope is in God forever.

132. God keeps His promises to David.

133. Unity among the brethren is pleasant and precious; a sweet smell.

134. Bless the Lord by night and day.

135. God deserves praise for destroying false gods and those who serve them.

136. His mercy endureth forever; Demonstrated by His creation and deliverance.

137. As captives in Babylon they could not sing but they could remember and pray.

138. God has magnified His Word above His name; He will revive and save me.

139. God knows all about me; He sees me; Search me and know me.

140. Deliver me from the traps of the wicked; Let them be destroyed with fire.

141. Hear my prayer; Let the righteous reprove me; Mine eyes are on Thee.

142. No man cared for my soul; Attend unto my cry.

143. No man is justified in God's sight; Lead in the way I walk; Teach me thy will.

144. Man is like unto vanity; Happy the people whose God is the Lord.

145. All Thy works shall praise Thee; He upholds all who fall; He preserves them.

146. Ten things God does for us; Put no trust in man.

147. God regathers Israel, the nation whom He has dealt with like no other.

148. Let every living being praise the Lord, for His excellent name and works.

149. Praise the King; He loves His people and defeats enemies with their sword.

150. Praise the Lord for His mighty acts with orchestra and chorus.

PROVERBS

"A proverb is a short statement based on long experience."

1. Learning objectives for the Proverbs; Choosing friends; Wisdom speaks.

   "It's what you learn after you know everything that counts." v. 1-7
   "If we fail to fear God, I fear we will fail Him." v. 29-32

2. Seek wisdom; it will preserve from the evil way and the strange woman.

3. Trust in the Lord; The merchandise of wisdom; The preservation of wisdom.

   *"Mercy and truth are more enduring because
   they are more endearing."* v. 3,4

4. The promotion of wisdom; Keep your heart, your eyes, your feet.

   *"Heart issues: Keep your heart, shut your mouth,
   look straight ahead, and think where you are going."* v. 23-27

5. Refuse the strange woman; Love your own wife; God is watching.

6. Consider your words; The ant, the naughty; What God hates; Wisdom in discerning women.

   *"A woman took down the most spiritual man (David),
   the smartest man (Solomon), and the strongest man (Samson)."*
   - Don Strange, Proverbs 6:23-29

7. The wiles of the strange woman with a young man.

   "The 'strange woman' is the woman who is off limits to you." v. 5

8. The instruction of wisdom: I was with God in the creation.

9. The wise woman speaks; The foolish woman speaks.

10. Contrasts between the wicked and the righteous.

11. Contrast between the upright and wicked; How they view life.

12. The wicked are overthrown, but the house of the righteous shall stand.

13. Differences between the wise and the foolish.

14. There is a way which seemeth right unto a man, but the end…death.

"Let's keep the ox and clean the crib" - Clarence Sexton   v. 4

15. Words and wisdom of the wise versus words and walk of the wicked.

"The heart teaches the mouth and work establishes the thoughts." v. 28; 16:3

16. Difference between the proud and the humble.

17. The power of our words for good or evil.

18. Life and death are in the power of the tongue.

19. Wisdom, discretion and the fear of the Lord.

20. Strife; The sluggard; Faithfulness; Boasting; The king.

21. The king's heart is in God's hand; The slothful; Sacrifice of the wicked.

22. Observations concerning rich and poor; Remove not the ancient landmark.

"God created us, but parents fashion us." v. 6

23. Behavior before a ruler; The wise son; Characteristic effects of wine.

24. Difference between wicked and wise; Respect of persons; Way of slothful.

25. Standing before a king; Those who offend others.

26. The fool; The slothful; The meddler; The talebearer.

27. Characteristics of a friend; Manage your finances.

28. Better are the humble than the rich; the righteous than the wicked.

29. Loving wisdom brings reward; Following foolishness brings heartache.

30. Who can comprehend God? There's a generation…; There are things wonderful, wise.

31. The virtuous woman; Kings ought not to drink wine.

ECCLESIASTES

1. Time passes and with it memories; Nothing new under the sun.

2. Vanity – mirth, wine, work, music, lust, amassing wealth, sleeplessness.

3. A time for everything; One dies as all die – animals and man.

4. Oppressors and oppressed; Being alone is vanity; Better to be poor and wise.

5. Be not rash with thy words; Use goods and riches wisely.

6. A rich man having it all and enjoying none of it is vanity.

7. Better to mourn than laugh; Wisdom and fear of God will preserve you.

8. The power of the king; The wicked and righteous both reap what they sow.

9. Life's event for all, end in death; Wisdom is better than strength.

10. A wise man's heart is at his right hand, but a fool's heart at his left.

11. Learn the lessons of the clouds, trees, wind, unborn, youth.

"It is an easy step from Contemporary to Charismatic. You fall in the direction which you lean." v. 3

12. Characteristics of the aged; Fear God and keep His commandments.

SONG OF SOLOMON

1. The bride describes her bridegroom and desires his love.

2. She describes how he loves her; She wants to go away with him.

3. She seeks but cannot find him; She describes his bed.

4. He describes her physical beauty; He is ravished with her love.

5. He comes by but leaves; She looks for him; She describes his body.

6. He describes her as his choice among the others. (Queens and concubines)

7. He explains his yearning and desire to love her; She is satisfied.

8. Love is strong as death; She lets him sleep; Her physical endowments bring favor.

ISAIAH

1. Isaiah calls the people to willing obedience from refusing and rebelling.

2. God will humble and judge the idolaters; their pride will be humbled.

3. Judgment includes women and children being rulers; Lose fancy ornaments.

4. Survivors will be helped by God from the heat and the cold.

5. Israel is the vineyard of the Lord; He knows their sins and will bring the enemy.

6. God calls Isaiah to preach; He is to preach till all are gone.

"Preach for results, but don't let your results
determine if you preach." v. 10

7. Isaiah prophesies destruction of Ahaz's enemies Syria/Samaria; Sign of virgin.

8. Isaiah's son Mahershalalhashbaz is a sign; Beware of false spirits.

9. God's hand against Israel for idolatry, hypocrisy; "unto us a child is born…"

10. God uses Assyria as His Rod on Israel; God will also punish Assyria.

11. Activities during the Millennium; Peace among animals and man.

12. During Millennium Israel will praise the Lord and God will comfort His people.

13. Prophecy concerning the destruction and desolation of Babylon.

14. Continued prophecy against Babylon; Judgment on Lucifer.

15. The burden of Moab; Their destruction.

16. Moab is proud, but God will judge from Jerusalem.

17. Burden against Damascus; City emptied; Idols forsaken, Nations destroyed.

18. Woe to Ethiopia.

19. Woe to Egypt; God will make them fight each other; They will serve the Lord.

20. Isaiah is naked and barefoot three years–sign of Assyria defeating Egypt and Ethiopia.

21. Watchman declares the destruction of Babylon, Dumah and Arabia.

22. Jerusalem eats and drinks instead of confessing and weeping during its demise.

23. Tyre is laid waste for 70 years. Restored to bring God glory.

24. Israel is emptied then filled; References to Tribulation, Armageddon and Millennium.

25. Song of praise; He is strength to poor, refuge from storm, shadow from heat.

26. Israel will sing a song of trust in God and deliverance; Resurrection will come.

27. Israel will be established; Egypt and Assyria shall worship God in Jerusalem.

28. God will teach His people doctrine, knowledge because they have erred.

    "We cannot make a covenant with death;
    we can only prepare for it." v.15

    "Mock not at Hell or Hell will mock at you." v. 18

    "You cannot rest on a lie or cover yourself with one." v. 20

29. Woe to Jerusalem; Ignorance will turn into wisdom; The poor will rejoice.

30. The ruin and restoration of Jerusalem.

    "God graciously waits for us until we learn to wait for Him." v. 18

31. Woe to those who trust in Egypt for help; they will cast away their idols.

32. The righteous king; The careless women; The peaceful people.

33. God will deliver His people; They will trust in Him; He is judge, lawgiver, king.

34. The sword of the Lord will devour His enemies; His people will seek His Word.

35. Israel will blossom as the rose; Sick will be healed; Ransomed will return.

36. Rabshakeh of Assyria mocks, threatens Hezekiah and people on the wall.

37. Hezekiah appeals to God for help; God smites 185,000; Sennacherib killed by sons.

38. Hezekiah healed of sickness with lump of figs; He praises the Lord.

39. Hezekiah shows Babylonian visitors his treasure; Isaiah predicts future plunder.

40. God will comfort His people; to whom will you liken God?

41. "Fear not, I will help thee"; Challenge to false religion.

42. Jesus, the servant, will bring judgment; He will shame those trusting in idols.

43. God, the redeemer will make Israel His witnesses.

44. God will bless His servant Israel; The foolish actions and beliefs of idolaters.

    "If you can make your own god, it didn't make you." v. 13-15

45. Things God has created: light and dark, salvation and righteousness, earth and heavens.

46. God knows the future as the past; Israel is His glory.

47. Doom upon Babylon for mistreating Israel; none will deliver them.

48. God judged Israel and used the furnace of affliction to reclaim them.

49. Servant's message to Israel and Gentiles; I have heard thee, I will not forget thee.

50. God will reclaim divorced Israel; prophesy of Jesus being smitten, spit on.

51. Deliverance of God will bring joy and song, comfort and redemption.

52. Israel redeemed; Beautiful feet; Rejected servant to sprinkle many nations.

> *"God has not left us to the mercy of a heart*
> *that wants its own way."* - Sellers v. 7

> *"There is no greater wrath than when God withholds His Word;*
> *no greater grace than when He gives it."* - Martin Luther v. 7

53. Suffering of the Servant and the Satisfaction of the Father.

> *"We ought to hate the sin that scourged our Savior."* v. 4

54. Heritage of God's servants; No weapon will prosper against thee; nor tongue.

55. God's thoughts and ways are higher than ours; God will accomplish His Word.

56. Injunction to do justice; Joy in the house of prayer; Lazy watchmen.

57. The righteous are taken from evil to come; God will restore the humble.

58. God desires fast of showing mercy; Delight in God's ways will get God's ear.

59. Iniquity caused God not to save or hear; Truth is fallen; God's standard will rise.

60. The regathering and future glory of Israel.

61. God will give Israel beauty for ashes; He will make them priests and ministers.

62. Israel will be called Hepzibah, Beulah, the holy people, redeemed, sought out.

63. Blood-sprinkled garments of wrath; God remembers past deliverances.

64. We pray for God to come down and forgive our sins – restore the wilderness.

65. How Israel provoked God; Their restoration – the Millennial period.

66. The proud destroyed, the humble restored; Armageddon, Millennium.

JEREMIAH

1. Jeremiah's call: time of it, manner of it, objection to it, promise concerning it.

2. Israel, why have you left the Lord to choose sin and vain gods? A lot of questions.

3. Israel is like an unfaithful wife who has forgotten the good of her husband.

> *"The root of backsliding is forgetting God."* v. 1-3

> *"A backslider must often live with the shame of the sin committed while in a back-slidden condition."* v. 22-25

4. Break up your fallow ground, circumcise yourselves, wash your heart. Get right with God.

5. Jerusalem refused to return; Iniquities have withheld good things; Enemy is coming.

> *"Israel in Babylon: They that served strange gods would now serve strangers in a strange land."* v. 19

6. Destruction is near for her sins and falsehood; They ignore the watchman.

7. They trust in lying words, hardened their neck – idolatry, robbery, adultery.

> *"It is a fearful thing when God will not hear your prayer."* v. 16

8. Backsliding: unrepentant, proud, covetous, deceived, no shame, religious formality.

9. Treachery among people; God delights in loving kindness, judgment and righteousness.

10. Don't make gods like heathen; It is not in man to direct his steps.

11. Obey so I can bless you; Men of Anathoth threaten Jeremiah for his prophecy.

12. Wicked enjoy their sin, but will be wearied in the day of captivity and war.

13. Israel is a marred girdle; Jeremiah weeps for the coming destruction.

14. God will not accept their prayers; Jeremiah intercedes for them.

15. Appointed to the sword, famine, captivity and death; deliverance if they return.

16. Don't get married or have children; they will be destroyed; God will restore Israel.

17. Don't trust the arm of flesh; Trust the Lord; Hallow the Sabbath day.

18. God is the potter, Israel the clay; They plot against Jeremiah.

19. The object lesson to Israel of the broken bottle.

"Israel was God's spiritual Humpty Dumpty." v. 11

20. Jeremiah rebukes Pashur and prophesies his demise; Jeremiah is depressed.

"Make every disappointment an opportunity to glorify God." v. 9

21. Jeremiah answers King Zedekiah that God Himself will fight against him.

22. To the king – Do right or be sent away; Doom of Jehoiakim and Jehoiachin.

23. Woe to pastors who scatter the flock; Profane prophet and priest reproached.

24. Vision of good figs and evil figs; Those spared and those slain by Babylonians.

25. Captivity to be 70 years; Surrounding nations bidden to drink the cup of wrath.

26. Plot against Jeremiah by the prophets and priests foiled by princes and people.

27. Bonds and yokes sent to nearby nations to drink the cup of God's wrath.

*"If you will not submit to God,
He may cause you to submit to the enemy."* v. 12

28. Hananiah falsely prophesies deliverance; Jeremiah prophesies his death.

29. Jeremiah writes to captives to stay and thrive; He curses three other false prophets.

30. God encourages suffering Israel with promise of eventual restoration.

31. God will restore people to the land with joy and singing; His new covenant.

32. Jeremiah in prison buys uncle's property as sign of future restoration to land.

33. Call unto me and I will show thee; The Lord our righteousness; Return from captivity.

*"God will not excite us with a prayer
He does not intend to answer."* v. 3

34. Zedekiah to be captured but spared; People release Jewish slaves, then enslave again.

35. Rechabites refuse to drink wine, but Israel will not obey God's servants.

36. King Zedekiah burns roll; Jeremiah rewrites it and more.

37. Jeremiah imprisoned; King inquires; Jeremiah pleads for his life but tells truth.

38. Jeremiah put in dungeon; Abedmelech takes him out; King asks Jeremiah's advice.

39. Zedekiah is captured and eyes put out; Jeremiah and Abedmelech are freed.

40. Jeremiah stays in the land; Gedaliah does not believe Ishmael is a threat.

41. Ishmael kills Gedaliah and Jews; Johanan delivers people; Returns to Jerusalem.

42. People ask Jeremiah what to do; He warns against going to Egypt for protection.

43. People rebelliously go to Egypt and take Jeremiah; He prophesies destruction by Babylon.

44. God will punish the proud in Egypt; Remnant shall return; Pharaoh to be captured.

*"As long as we forget, God remembers;
when we remember, God forgets."* v. 9

*"People think that because the economy is good,
God doesn't care if they serve their own gods.
They misinterpret His patience for His permission."* v. 17

45. Jeremiah warns Baruch not to seek things for himself; His life to be spared.

46. God to make full end of nations, but not Israel; though not unpunished.

47. Sword of the Lord will be against the Philistines.

48. Moab is destroyed because of pride, arrogance and haughtiness of heart.

49. Ammon is conquered for pride and trust in high places; Eventually restored.

50. Babylon to be spoiled and made desolate by a northern army (Medo-Persia).

51. Babylon brought low for her idolatries; Seraiah, the quiet prince; Book sinks.

52. Account of Zedekiah's demise and Jeremiah's destruction; Captives; King Jehoiachin well-treated.

LAMENTATIONS

1. Lamenting the destruction of God's people because of sin. "Is it nothing to you?"

2. God is the enemy; The prophets have no vision; The enemies rejoice.

3. God's mercies fail not; Let us return to the Lord; God will destroy my enemies.

> *"God's Character demands His faithfulness,*
> *His Consistency determines His faithfulness*
> *and His Care demonstrates His faithfulness."* v. 22-26

4. Description of starvation; Sins of prophets and priests is revisited.

5. Persecution and suffering under the hand of the enemy because of sin.

EZEKIEL

"The phrase, 'and they shall know that I am the Lord'
is mentioned 78 times in Ezekiel."

1. Vision of four creatures with four faces, with four wheels; Vision of throne and glory of God.

2. Ezekiel is chosen and sent to prophesy to Israel, the rebellious house.

3. Ezekiel eats roll (Word of God) to speak to people; Comes to the captives as a watchman.

4. He portrays the siege of Jerusalem with tile; Makes bread baked with dung for 390 days.

5. Ezekiel's hair to show judgment: one-third die with pestilence; one-third die with the sword; one-third are scattered.

6. God's heart broken with their whorish heart; Their scattering; Remnant are preserved.

7. Israel will reap what it sowed; Mischief and rumor will plague them.

8. Vision of idolatrous ancients in Temple worshiping sun; God is angry.

   "God is loath to leave us, but is ready to return." Ch. 8-11; 43

9. Vision of six men: one marking the righteous; five slaying the wicked; Ezekiel intercedes.

10. Vision of the coals, the cherubims and glory of God leaving Temple.

11. Prophecy against Pelatiah and false prophets; He dies; God is their sanctuary.

12. Ezekiel moves his stuff, sign of captivity; The people do not believe.

13. Woe to false prophets who prophecy lies unto which the innocent trust.

14. God opposes idols in their hearts; Neither Noah, Daniel nor Job can deliver them.

> *"Noah, man of promise; Daniel, man of purity;*
> *Job, man of patience."* v. 14

15. God will devour Jerusalem as a man burns a useless vine in a fire.

16. Lowly origin of Israel; Used beauty to prostitute herself; Destroyed by lovers.

> *"Weak-hearted women abandon their husbands and children."* v. 30,45

> *"Sodom's downfall caused by pride, prosperity,*
> *plenty of time, poor ignored."* v.49

17. Two eagles and the vine: sign of Babylonians plucking up Israel and God restoring her.

18. Children shall not pay for the sins of their fathers; Soul that sinneth shall die.

> *"God does not hold us accountable for the sins of our fathers*
> *unless we follow in them."* v. 19-23

19. Israel, like a young lion, is captured and taken to Babylon.

20. Elders inquire of Ezekiel; Message of judgment; Future repentance and restoration.

21. Babylon is God's sharpened sword on Israel and Ammon.

22. Their sins: oppression, sexual sins, conspiracy, thievery; No advocate found.

> *"God exposes the sins of the prophets, priests, princes and people."*

23. Harlotry of Aholah and Aholibah; Their punishment for spiritual adultery.

24. Ezekiel's wife dies; He does not mourn; Sign of coming Temple destruction.

25. God will judge Ammon, Moab, Edom, Philistines for hurting Israel during Babylonian captivity.

26. Tyre will be ruined for mocking and rejoicing at the fall of Jerusalem.

27. Lamentation for Tyre; Destruction of its trade, fairs, wealth and merchants.

28. Prince of Tyre's demise for thinking himself God. King of Tyrus is Lucifer.

29. Egypt will be empty for 40 years; then will return; Said they made the Nile.

30. Babylon will come on Egypt to destroy it.; The king's arm will be broken.

31. Egypt's warning: like Assyria, large, beautiful tree, cut down, destroyed; so are ye.

"Hell is down in the earth."
(See 31:14,16,17,18; 32:23,24,25,27,29,30).)

32. Egypt's end with others will be graves in the sides of the pit, nether parts.

33. Ezekiel is the watchman to warn; The people hear but don't do.

34. Shepherds of Israel are cruel; God will raise up His shepherd David; Showers of blessing.

35. Mount Seir (Edom) will be punished for their pride against God.

36. God's promise to restore Israel to the land and give a new heart for His glory.

37. Valley of dry bones; Two sticks: Israel and Judah will be one again.

38. Northern confederacy will come against Israel; God will destroy them.

39. Gog will invade Israel and be destroyed; Israel will bury for seven months.

40. The man with measuring rod measures courts, chambers and gates.

41. Measuring of the Temple, courts and chambers; Palms and cherubim.

42. The holy chambers where priests eat the holy offerings; Place for garments.

43. The glory of God returns; Israel shown House to make them ashamed, consecrated.

   "Seeing God's house causes people to be ashamed of their iniquity." v. 10

44. They are not to profane the Temple; Rules and guidelines for the priests.

45. Apportioned land for priests; Just measures; The prince's offering.

46. Rules for the offerings; Places for boiling the sacrifices for the priests.

47. Healing waters, lined with fruit trees; Good fishing; Leaves for healing.

48. Divisions of the land; Portions for tribes, priests, city, prince; city gates.

DANIEL

1. Daniel and friends purpose not to defile themselves; God honors them with wisdom.

   "You can change your name but not your nature." v. 7-8
   "Melzar proved Daniel and Daniel proved God." v. 12-15
   "Daniel was honored because he honored God." v. 19-20

2. Daniel interprets and reveals the king's dream of a great image.

3. Nebuchadnezzar's image of gold is worshiped by all; Shadrach, Meshech, and Abednego delivered from fire.

> *"Stand, if you have to stand alone, but stand." Dan. 3:12*

> *"The three Hebrew children: No burning - No blessing; No Trial - No Triumph." v. 25*

4. Nebuchadnezzar's dream of cut tree comes to pass; King like a beast for seven years; Restored.

5. Belshazzar sees writing on the wall; Daniel interpretation; King slain by Medes.

6. Daniel delivered from den of lions; King glorifies God; Enemies slain by lions.

> *"I would rather fail in a cause that will ultimately succeed, than succeed in a cause that will ultimately fail." v. 17*

7. Vision of four beasts – world kingdoms; Explanation of Antichrist.

8. Vision of Ram (Medo-Persia) and Goat (Greece), then Antichrist in last days.

9. Daniel understands Jeremiah; 70 years captivity; Messiah cut off; Antichrist breaks covenant.

10. Daniel greatly beloved; Gabriel detained by Prince of Persia; gives message.

11. Vision of conflicts between kings of North and South; Antiochus/Antichrist destroyed.

12. Time of Jacob's trouble three and one-half years; Many purified, Others perish; Daniel is at peace.

HOSEA

1. Hosea marries Gomer, has three children; Sign of judgment to Israel.

2. Hosea calls back his wife from adultery as God calls Israel back.

3. Hosea buys back his wife to be faithful; Israel will return to seek God.

4. Because they forgot God, God will forget their children.

> *"A lack of knowledge is directly related
> to knowledge that is rejected." v. 6*

5. They will seek God in affliction but not find Him; No deliverance from Assyria.

6. God invites them to return, though they have dealt treacherously with Him.

7. Ephraim is a cake not turned, as a silly dove without heart, a deceitful bow.

8. They have sown the wind and will reap the whirlwind, forgotten their Maker.

9. Their food shall fail; They are scattered and wander among the nations.

10. Israel an empty vine; Judgment springs up like hemlock; Time to seek the Lord.

11. God wooed Ephraim; They refused to return; He will restore; Judah is faithful.

12. Jacob had power with God; God spoke by prophets (Jacob, Moses, others).

13. Ephraim forgot God and served Baal; God will destroy, yet ransom them.

14. God's promise to restore the penitent, heal, revive; His ways are right.

JOEL

1. Pestilence brings famine; Day of the Lord causes loss and lamentation.

2. From retribution to repentance, to restoration; prophecy of Acts 2.

3. Tribulation – God calls nations to battle in the valley; Israel blessed in Millennium.

AMOS

1. God visits the transgressions of Damascus, Gaza, Tyrus, Edom and Ammon.

2. God visits the transgressions of Moab, Judah and Israel.

3. Seven rhetorical questions: God will deliver but a remnant.

4. God rebukes sarcastically; lack of rain, bread, crops; Prepare to meet God.

5. God begs them to seek Him for their own good; Hates their feasts and sacrifices.

6. Trust not in surrounding nations; God will bring upon them a nation to destroy.

7. Plague of grasshoppers and fire; Priest Amaziah tells king about Amos; To flee.

8. Basket of summer fruit spells the end; A famine of hearing the Word of God.

9. Wicked cannot escape; God will restore Israel again to fruitfulness.

OBADIAH

1. Vision against Edom (Esau) for their pride and mistreatment of Israel (Jacob).

JONAH

1. Jonah runs and is thrown overboard.

    Prodigal Prophet/ Running/ Paid

2. Jonah prays from fish's belly.

    Praying Prophet/ Turning/ Prayed

3. Jonah preaches; Ninevites repent.

    Preaching Prophet/ Walking/ Obeyed

    "Jonah - A prophet who enjoyed the message but not the results." 3:4;4:3

4. Jonah complains though blessed.

    Pouting Prophet/ Sulking/ Dismayed

MICAH

1. Warning to Samaritans and Jerusalem of future destruction and captivity.

2. Wealthy imagine and practice oppression; They will believe false prophets.

3. Woe: princes pluck skin; Prophets say "peace" for money; Priests teach for hire.

4. Millennium: no more war; into Babylon then returned; Israel will rule.

5. Jesus from Bethlehem; Jacob to destroy enemies and their gods.

6. God's controversy with Israel; God requires justice, mercy, humility.

7. Look to God, not undependable man; God pardons iniquity; Casts sins into sea.

NAHUM

1. God will destroy Nineveh, yet God is good, a stronghold in the day of trouble.

2. God will empty Nineveh and take her prey and make her desolate.

3. Nineveh reaps what she sowed: military, economic destruction for idolatries.

HABAKKUK

1. The prophet asks, "Why use wicked Babylon to devour more righteous Israel?"

2. God judges pride, greed, coveting, drunkenness, idolatry; Just shall live by faith.

3. Prayer: revive thy work, drive out the enemy, God is just, God is my strength.

ZEPHANIAH

1. God will consume the land and people for their idolatry and apathy.

   "If Satan has half, he will have all; if the Lord has but half,
   He will have none." v. 4-5

2. Seek righteousness for mercy; Woe on Philistines, Moab, Ammon, Ninevites.

3. Woe to the filthy and oppressing city (Jerusalem); Destroyed, then restored.

HAGGAI

1. Haggai calls the people to rebuild the Temple; Blessing held back till it begins.

2. The people rebuild, blessing returns; God's glory makes this Temple greater.

   "It is more important what is in the house
   than what the house looks like." v.7-9

ZECHARIAH

1. Turn from evil ways; Four horns that scatter Israel; Four carpenters destroy horns.

2. Even in judgment Israel is the apple of His eye.

3. Satan rebuked, Joshua cleansed and clothed; The BRANCH will be revealed.

4. Zerubbabel will finish Temple; Two olive trees – two anointed ones.

5. The flying scroll – curse on thieves and liars; Ephah – house built in Shinar.

6. Four horses – quiet the heathen, release the captives; The BRANCH will rule.

7. Israel had refused to listen; hence, God refused to hear their cries.

8. God loves and will restore Israel; Foreigners will seek to follow the Jew.

9. Prophecy against Philistines; Zion's humble king on an ass; God saves Judah.

10. The latter rain; Judah is strengthened; Scattered and gathered.

11. Beauty & Bands (Israel and Judah); Evil shepherds destroyed; Thirty pieces of silver.

12. All nations against Israel; God destroys them at Megiddo.

13. Wounded in the house of his friends; Smite the shepherd, sheep will scatter.

14. Jesus comes to Mt. of Olives with saints to destroy enemies and set up King.

MALACHI

1. Israel questions God's love; Deny their polluted sacrifices; Deceiver cursed.

2. Priests caused corruption and stumbling; Judah is idolatrous; Calling evil good.

3. God's refiner's fire; Robbing in tithes and offerings; Book of remembrance.

4. Righteous tread down the wicked; Coming of Elijah (John the Baptist).

NEW TESTAMENT

MATTHEW

1. Genealogy of Jesus, Abraham to Joseph; Joseph told to take Mary.

2. Wise men worship Jesus; Herod kills Bethlehem babies; Return from Egypt.

3. John the Baptist warns Pharisees and Sadducees; Baptizes Jesus; Spirit descends on Jesus.

4. Jesus tempted; John jailed, Jesus preaches; Calls four disciples; Heals and preaches.

5. Beatitudes; Sermon on the Mount; Salt and light; Letter and spirit of Law.

"Anything good from us is what God does in us." v. 16

"Jesus is the Sun; since we reflect His light
that makes us spiritual moonshine." v. 14

6. When you give, pray, fast…; Lord's prayer; True treasure; Trust in God.

7. Judge not; Ask, seek, knock; Narrow and broad way; Inspect fruit; Hear and do.

"I'm walking on a broad path on the Narrow way (I'm free);
The lost are walking in a narrow path on the broad way.
(bound by drugs, lust, etc.)" - Don Strange v. 13-14

"We think we live in the land of the living on our way to the land
of the dying; but really, we are in the land of the dying
on the way to the land of the living." - Don Strange v. 13-14

"Religion without Christ is spiritual inoculation
- getting a little bit of it to keep from getting the real thing." v.21-23

"Every right church and good home are built on doctrine."
- Paul Chappell v. 24-27

8. Centurion, great faith; Disciples in storm, Little faith; Gadarenes, no faith.

"The disciples had faith to follow Jesus
but not to trust Him in the storm." v. 23-26

"The devil-possessed was a Nude Dude in a Rude Mood." v. 28-34

"This chapter illustrates great faith v. 10,
little faith v. 26, and no faith v. 34."

9. Palsied healed; Matthew called; Preaching and healing; Compassion on the multitude.

"The harvest in Jesus' day was 150 million;
today it is over 7 billion." v. 36-37

"Concerning the lost: See what Jesus saw, Feel what Jesus felt,
Say what Jesus said, and Do what Jesus did." v. 36-38

10. Call and instruction of the Twelve; Cost and rewards of service.

"Don't depend on past experience
for present expression or future expectation." 9-15

"If we have quality we will have quantity. We then need
to train the quantity into quality." - Gary Furnish v. 19-28

11. John the Baptist jailed, discouraged, doubting; Praised by Jesus; Come unto me.

12. Plucked grain on Sabbath; Jesus heals on Sabbath; House divided; Seeking Signs.

"To reject what the Holy Ghost says about Christ
is to refuse Christ as Savior." v. 31

13. Parable of the sower, wheat and tares, mustard seed, etc; Jesus' brothers, Sisters.

> *"Jesus came to the masses to reach a man;*
> *then He uses the man to reach the masses."* v. 1-11

14. John beheaded; Feeding of 5,000; Jesus and Peter walk on water.

15. Tradition or true worship; Syro-Phonecian daughter healed; Feeding of 4,000.

> *"It is better to have a heart without words,*
> *than having words without heart."* v. 8

> *"Are you waiting on God or are you making God wait?"*
> -Dan Knickerbocker v.22-28

16. Leaven of the Pharisees; Peter's confession; Peter rebuked; Discipleship.

> *"Red sky in morning, sailors take warning; Red sky at night,*
> *sailor's delight."* v. 2-3

> *"I - Person, Will - Pace, Build - Pain, My - Possession,*
> *Church - Product"* v. 18

> *"Jesus didn't say that He would build my church*
> *or that I would build His church."*

17. Transfiguration; This kind goeth out by prayer and fasting; Tribute money found in mouth of fish.

18. Come as little children; The ninety and nine; Forgive seventy times seven, as you have been forgiven.

> *"Forgiveness is releasing someone from a debt they owe you."* v. 28

19. Marriage, divorce and celibacy; Rich young ruler; Reward of faithfulness.

20. Laborers paid what was right; Jesus, the example of ministering; Blind healed.

> *"God is not "fair"; He is right."* - Tim Knickerbocker v. 1-16

21. Triumphal entry; Cleansing the Temple; Fig tree cursed; Two sons; Evil vineyard men.

"We are either religious before men or righteous before God." v. 28-32

22. Wedding supper; Render unto Caesar; Jesus silences questions of Pharisees and Sadducees.

23. Woe to scribes and Pharisees for their hypocrisy; Jesus pleads for Jerusalem.

24. Signs of the Tribulation and return of Christ; Watch, be ready, Live godly.

25. Ten virgins; Servants and talents; Serving the least of these.

26. Mary anoints Jesus; Passover and the Lord's Supper; Gethsemane; Judas' kiss; Peter's denial.

"Judas Iscariot kissed the door of Heaven but died and went to Hell." 26:49, 27:5

27. Judas dies; Jesus before Pilate; Mocked, crucified; Veil rent; Jesus buried.

28. He is risen! Attempted cover-up; Great Commission; Ascension.

"If you refuse to believe the truth, you will believe a lie." v. 13-15

MARK

1. John the Baptist; Jesus baptized; Chooses disciples; Jesus preaches and heals.

2. Man borne of four healed; Levi called; Jesus eats with sinners; Man and Sabbath.

"What the four friends did who helped their sick friend to Jesus was inconvenient, unconventional and costly." - Simon Watts, England

3. Healing on Sabbath; Twelve ordained; House divided; Jesus' true mother and brethren.

> *"God chooses us to be with Him and then to send us forth."* v. 14

4. Teaching by sea; Purpose of parables; Parable of sower, candle; Sea calmed.

> *"How we respond to what we hear*
> *determines if God will give us more."* v. 24

5. Demoniac restored; Woman with issue of blood; Jairus' daughter raised from the dead.

> *"The Devil had the demoniac in isolation,*
> *humiliation and rebellion."*

> *"In this chapter Jesus demonstrated his power over*
> *the devil, death and disease."*

6. No honor in His own country; The Twelve sent; John beheaded; Feeds 5,000; Walks on water.

> *"Never assess your problem in light of your own resources."*
> - Don Strange v. 37-42

7. Ceremonial and real defilement; Syro-Phonecian daughter and deaf-mute healed.

> *"Man thinks he is defiled by food;*
> *God thinks we are defiled by thoughts."* v. 18-23

8. Feeding the 4,000; blind man healed; Peter confessed; Is rebuked; Discipleship.

> *"A faith that does not change your life*
> *is a faith that will not save your soul."* v. 35-36

> *"Three things you cannot afford to lose: your soul, your life, your*
> *testimony."* - Don Green v. 34-38

9. Transfiguration; deaf/dumb spirit cast out; Who is greatest? Giving offense.

10. Marriage and divorce; Blessed children; Rich young ruler; Blind Bartimaeus.

   "Salvation is not easy, but it is simple." v. 17-27

11. Triumphal Entry; Cursed fig tree; Cleansed temple; Pray believing; Jesus is questioned.

12. Wicked vineyard men; Render to Caesar; Whose wife? Greatest Commandment; Who is Christ?

13. Signs of the end; Tribulation; Second Coming; Injunction to Watch.

14. Mary anoints Jesus; Passover/Lord's Supper; Judas betrays; Peter's denial.

15. Jesus' trial; crucifixion, witnesses to His death; His burial.

16. Resurrection and appearances; Apostles commissioned; Ascension.

   "A Mission's Conference without Christ is a Missing Conference."
   -Edilberto Donizia, Philippino pastor v. 19-20

LUKE

1. Gabriel appears to Zacharias about John; Appears to Mary about Jesus.

2. Jesus born; Shepherds see him; Simeon, Anna see him; Twelve years old at Jerusalem.

   "Simeon and Anna - Two senior saints who saw the Savior." v. 25-38

3. Preaching of John the Baptist; Imprisoned; Genealogy of Jesus (from Joseph to Adam).

4. Jesus tempted; Preaches in Nazareth; Heals Peter's mother-in-law; Casts out demons.

5. Calls four disciples; Heals palsied man borne of four; Calls Levi; Teaches disciples.

6. Plucking corn and healing on Sabbath; Chose the Twelve; Sermon on Mount; The wise and the foolish.

> *"Three kinds of people in the church: Savers, spenders and sowers.*
> *Sowers are the only ones who invest in missions."*
> - Cham McMillen v. 38

7. Centurion's great faith; Son in Nain raised; John doubts; Sinner anoints Jesus.

8. Parables of: sower, candle; Sea stilled; The Gadarene; Issue stopped; Jairus' Daughter healed.

9. Sends the Twelve; Feeds 5,000; Transfiguration; Child delivered from devil; Discipleship.

10. Sends the Seventy; The Good Samaritan; Mary and Martha.

> *"GROWTH - God Reaching Others With These Hands."* v. 30-37

> *"Lord, keep on my heart what You have on Yours."*
> - Preston Griffis v. 33

> *"Martha was cumbered with physical activity;*
> *Mary was concerned with spiritual necessity."* v. 38-42

11. Lord's Prayer; House divided; Woe to Scribes, Pharisees, Lawyers.

> *"We need a revival of prayer before we can pray for revival."*
> - Jack Meeks v. 1

12. Fear God, not enemies; Beware of covetousness; Watch for His coming.

> *"Coveteousness is not wanting more, but keeping what God*
> *wants us to give away."* - Cham McMillen v. 15-21

13. Dung fig tree; Infirm woman; Kingdom like mustard seed, leaven; Strait gate.

14. Humility takes lower seat, calls poor to feast, crucifies self, forsakes all.

> *"To be a disciple there will be controls, conflict, confrontation,*
> *convictions, constraints, contributions and corrections."*
> - Don Green v. 33

15. Parables of lost sheep, lost coin, lost son (all reclaimed).

> *"The prodigal's father did not celebrate his son's sin,*
> *but rejoiced in his repentance."* v. 23-32

16. Unjust steward; God and mammon; Rich man and Lazarus.

> *"People use the word "hell" to show how tough they are,*
> *but there are no tough people in hell."* v. 23-24

> *"Hell" is the most mentioned and least believed-in place."* v. 31

> *"You cannot get a man out of hell, but you can help keep him out."*
> - Jerry Nye v. 26

> *"Three things the man in hell wanted but was refused:*
> *mercy, water, prayer."* v.24,27

17. Forgive seventy times seven; Servant's duty; Ten lepers cleansed; As it was in the days of Noah.

> *"Ten cleansed men: The ten had faith,*
> *but only one had appreciation."* v. 17

18. Unjust judge; Pharisee and Publican pray; Rich young ruler; Jericho blind man.

> *"Self-righteous people always despise others*
> *who are not like themselves."* v. 11

19. Zacchaeus; Parable of the ten pounds; Triumphal Entry; Cleansing the Temple.

    "Jesus' last commandment should be our first concern." v. 10

20. Husbandman and Son; Render to Caesar; Wife of seven; Christ, David's son.

21. Signs of the end time; Watch and pray.

22. Passover; Warning to disciples; Arrested in Mt. of Olives; Peter's denial.

23. Jesus before Pilate and Herod; Crucifixion; Joseph buries Jesus.

    "Malefactor" - "mal"= evil; "factor=factory - A factory of evil." v. 39

    *"No one has ever done more wrong against you
    than you have done against Christ,
    and yet He forgave you."* Luke 23:34

24. Resurrection of Christ; Two on way to Emmaus; Jesus appears in upper room; Ascension.

    "Whenever you hear a lie, look for the truth, it's nearby." v. 19-24

JOHN

1. Relation of John to Jesus; Jesus baptized; Andrew tells Peter; Philip, Nathan.

    *"Don't look for contradictions in the Bible, look for revelation."
    - Dick Riley* v. 1,14

    *"Salvation is of God: He thought it, bought it,
    taught it and I caught it!"*

2. Marriage at Cana; Cleansing the Temple; "Destroy this Temple…" , Miracles.

    "Fill your water pots and let God do the rest." v. 7-10

3. Nicodemus; John's opinion of Jesus' ministry.

"The Bible is the greatest book ever written, telling the greatest story ever told, about the greatest life ever lived." - Pastor Wheeler v.16

"The God of love, gave the Gift of love so I could enjoy the Guarantee of love." v. 16

"Everlasting life is a different life, a divine life and a delightful life."

4. Woman at the well; Nobleman's son healed at the seventh hour.

"The where of worship is not as important as the Who of worship." v. 20-24

"Woman learned that Jesus was: a Jew, greater than Jacob, a prophet, the Christ."

5. Lame man healed at pool of Bethesda; Work, witness of Christ; Search the Scriptures.

"Don't seek God's will for your life, give your life for God's will." -Lee Roberson v. 30

6. Feeding of the five thousand; Jesus walks on sea; Bread of life; Many disciples leave Jesus.

7. Brother's disbelieve; Jesus is called a devil; Seek to kill him; Nicodemus defends him.

"Christ will withdraw from those who drive Him from them." v. 1

8. Woman taken in adultery; Light of the world; True Jew; before Abraham, I AM.

"Believers have not just a changed life, but an exchanged life." v. 10-11

9. Blind man healed: is questioned, reviled, cast out; believes on Christ.

"People easily doubt that which they cannot reasonably explain." v. 13-34

10. The Good Shepherd; Jesus escapes a stoning; Claims to be God.

11. Death and resurrection of Lazarus; Prophecy of Caiaphas; Death plot for Jesus.

"Lazarus was loosed from his clothes, but Jesus left His." v. 44; 20:5-7

12. Mary anoints Jesus; Triumphal Entry; Discipleship; Man put out of synagogue.

"In relation to your own life: In loving, you lose; in hating, you win." v. 25

13. Jesus washes feet; Passover; A New Commandment.

"Basin theology" - wash your hands and other's feet." v. 4-5

14. Promise of a mansion; Ask; Love me-keep commands; Promise of Comforter.

15. Abide in the vine; Fruitfulness; Friends; Hated without a cause.

"When you become a Christian you should only do those things which become a Christian." - Cook v. 7-8

"A black preacher said, 'If you is what you was, you ain't!'" - Don Strange v. 16

"The cleaner the world looks, the dirtier I am." v. 19

16. Comforter is Promised: reproves, guides, glorify Christ, teacher; Overcomers.

"The Father gives to the Son who shows it to the Spirit, who shows it to the saint, who shows it to the sinner." v. 14-15

"There is no painless way to follow Jesus Christ." v. 33

17. Jesus' High Priestly Prayer.

"Believers recognize the glory of God in each other." v. 22

18. Jesus arrested, examined; Peter's denial; Jesus before Pilate.

> *"We will either deny ourselves or deny Christ."* v. 15-27

19. Jesus scourged though "no fault"; Crucifixion; Words from the Cross; Burial.

20. Mary at the tomb; Peter and John at tomb; Appearances; Mary; Upper room.

21. Appearance to disciples fishing; "Lovest thou me?" "Follow me."

ACTS

1. Ascension of Jesus, Matthias replaces Judas; Disciples wait in upper room.

> *"The cleaner the world looks to me,*
> *the dirtier I am. (and visa versa)"*

2. Pentecost; tongues; Peter's message; 3,000 saved, baptized, added, shared.

> *"A Biblical church is Scriptural, sociable, strong, solid,*
> *Sacrificial, soul winning, and a source of joy to all."* v. 41-47

3. Peter and John heal lame man; Crowd gathers; Peter preaches again.

> *"Great opportunities come by using well the small opportunities."* v. 1-6

4. Peter and John in prison; speak boldly, are threatened, filled with the Spirit, preached.

> *"First church: supplications went up, Spirit came down,*
> *saints went out and sinners came in."* Acts 4:31-37

5. Ananias and Sapphira lie and die; People healed; Apostles in prison, released by an angel.

6. Deacons appointed; Stephen preaches, is resisted; face shines like angel.

"The devoted deacon is filled with the Spirit, faith and power." v. 3-8

7. Stephen's sermon before Council; Stephen rejected and stoned; he forgives.

*"Stephen - They didn't just stone him to death,
they rocked him to sleep."* v. 56-60

*"About Guilt: Either blame yourself and repent,
or blame others and resist."* v. 57

"Trouble always follows truth." v.54-60

8. Burial of Stephen; Philip preaches and heals; Simon the sorcerer; Ethiopian Eunuch is saved.

9. Conversion of Saul; Preaches in Damascus; Escapes in basket; Dorcas raised from dead.

*"Paul - The Jewish terrorist who became a Christian.
From persecutor to propagator; from proud to humble."*

10. Peter's vision; Conversion of Cornelius; Tongues again; Cornelius baptized.

11. Peter's report to Jerusalem Christians; Scattered and preaching; Relief for famine.

12. James killed; Peter delivered from prison; Herod eaten of worms.

13. Paul and Barnabas first missionaries; Elymas blinded; Sermon at Antioch of Pisidia.

*"In our world today there are 250 countries, 6,500 language groups,
and 305 cities of over one million people each."*

*"In the Antioch church there was cooperation, occupation,
propagation, preparation, delegation and separation"*
v. 1-4 - Tim Knickerbocker

14. Iconium division; cripple healed; Paul and Barnabas worshiped, stoned, raised; Report to church in Antioch.

    "The ministry is not all we do for God, but all God does with us."
    14:27; 15:4,12

15. Jerusalem council; Report to Gentile believers; Contention between Paul and Barnabas.

    "Salvation is not a Jewish idea or a Gentile idea,
    but a Jesus idea." v. 1-11

16. Macedonian Call; Paul and Silas in Philippian jail; Church established in Philippi.

    "The jailer washed away the blood of persecution;
    Jesus washed the jailer in the blood of redemption;
    Paul washed the jailer in the waters of baptism." v. 33-34

17. Thessalonian riot; Noble Bereans; Idolatrous Athenians; Altar to Unknown God.

    "The people of Athens were religious,
    intellectual and accommodating." v. 16-21 - Simon Watts, England

18. Aquila and Priscilla; Paul in Corinth 1½ years; In Ephesus; Apollos helps.

    "God's promise gives confidence and results in continuance." v. 9-11

19. Disciples of John the Baptist baptized; Miracles; Seven sons of Sceva; goddess Diana.

    "Paul cast out demons, but the demons cast out the men." v. 12-16

    "If you must speak for your god, your god cannot speak for you;
    if you must defend your god, your god cannot defend you." v. 28-36

    "Ephesians were politically correct
    until they were Biblically in check." v. 28-36

20. Paul in Greece for three months; Eutychus raised; Paul's farewell to leaders.

    "When the routine gets rough, the resolve must be tough." v. 22-24

    "You cannot plant it if you eat it; we are either getters or givers."
    -Cham McMillen v. 35

21. Agabus' prophecy; Paul mobbed at Jerusalem; Delivered by soldiers; Asks to speak.

22. Paul's defense to people; Gives testimony; Escapes a scourging.

23. Paul before Sanhedrin; Divided over resurrection; Warned and delivered of a conspiracy.

24. Paul accused by Tertullus; Answers for himself to Felix; Felix expects bribe.

25. Paul before Festus; Appeals to Caesar; Festus finds no fault.

26. Paul before Agrippa; Gives testimony; Almost persuaded; Paul declares his innocence.

27. Euroclydon; Shipwreck; People are saved and escape to land.

28. Miracle snake bite; Ministry to Publius; Speaks to Roman Jews; In Rome for two years.

ROMANS

1. Paul plans to visit believers in Rome God's wrath to ungodly who choose sin.

2. Let God be judge; Law of conscience; The true Jew – circumcised in heart.

    "Justification - to be declared righteous before God because of faith in Christ" v.26

3. All have sinned; Justification precludes boasting; Law established, not eliminated.

   "You cannot have good unless you have God." v. 23-2

4. Righteousness through faith; Abraham's righteousness imputed by faith.

5. Justification by faith brings peace with God and access to grace; Where sin abounds grace much more abounds.

   "Old master brought sin and death;
   New master brings grace and life." v. 21

6. Buried and raised with Christ; Yield your members; Fruit of sin and holiness; Wages of sin.

   "Thankfulness says, 'I have much more than I deserve.'
   Unthankfulness says, 'I deserve much more than I have.'" v. 17

7. Dead to Law, married to Christ; Purpose of commandments; Law of old nature

8. No condemnation; The carnal and spiritual mind; Spirit witness; Conquerors in Christ.

   "Your walk does not determine your salvation; rather,
   your salvation determines your walk." v. 1

   "I asked, 'Lord give me all things that I may enjoy life.'
   God gave me life so I could enjoy all things." v. 28

9. Paul's burden for Jews; True sons of Abraham; God chooses vessels of honor and dishonor.

   "Election is God choosing those who choose Him,
   knowing who would choose." v. 23-24

10. Zeal without knowledge; Beautiful gospel feet; Faith cometh by hearing the Word.

"At the end of the Ten Commandments you will find only Jesus." v. 4

"They will not know, they must be sought; they will not come they must be brought; they will not learn, they must be taught; Satan hinders, he must be fought." - Pete Knickerbocker v. 14-15

11. God not done with Israel; Spiritually blind; Grafted in again; O the depth of the riches of Christ.

12. Proper relationship to God, to the brethren, to your enemies.

> *"Grace is the divine influence on the heart and its reflection in the life."* v. 6

13. Citizen's responsibility to government; Walk honestly in these last days.

14. Do not judge others in debatable matters; Do not be a stumbling block.

> *"Discouragement is lack of courage, because of lack of trust in God, which is lack of faith, which is sin."* -Gary Furnish v. 23

15. Strong are to help weak; Reaching the Gentiles; Contribution to poor saints.

> *"We look for souls because we love God who loves souls."* v. 16

16. Paul - Help my helpers in the ministry; Avoid divisive people; Give gospel to all nations.

I CORINTHIANS

1. Church corrected for divisions and contentions; God chooses foolish things.

"The state of the saints - God's Salvation in us, Christ's testimony from us, and God's faithfulness to us." v. 4-9

2. Paul's preaching done with power not deception; Spirit teaches things of God.

> *"If I fear man, I avoid him; if I fear God I get closer to Him."* v. 3

3. Three kinds: natural, spiritual, carnal men; Works tried by fire; Glory in the Lord.

> *"We are needed for the planting and watering,*
> *but God is needed for the increase."* v.6

> *"Our work for Christ is communicated,*
> *evaluated, and rewarded."* v. 11-13

4. Stewards to be faithful; not puffed up; Paul's sufferings; Shall I come with a rod or with love?

5. Purge out the fornicator; Do not fellowship with sinning brethren.

6. Do not go to law against a brother; Our bodies are temple of Holy Spirit, not for fornication.

7. Guidelines for marriage; Jew and Gentile circumcision; Virgins; The married.

8. Eating meat offered to idols; Liberty and conscience in doing so.

> *"Our Christian liberty is limited by love."*

9. The rights of an apostle, willingly relinquished for the gospel's sake; The prize.

> *"What you believe is what you become, is to whom you belong*
> *and determines how you behave."* v. 19-23

> *"If you don't tell your body what to do, your body will tell*
> *you what to do."* - Dan Knickerbocker v. 27

10. Israel's history is example to warn; Eat, asking no questions; Do all for God's glory.

11. Order of authority: God, Christ, man, woman; Hair is for a covering; Taking the Lord's Supper.

12. Spiritual gifts; Given by Spirit, different, tempered; Priority of preaching and teaching.

13. Spiritual gifts to be practiced with charity; Charity never fails; it is the greatest.

    "Love is identified or known by the action that moves it."

14. Preaching is greater than tongues; Seek to edify; Tongues must be interpreted; Women to be silent.

    "The 'Why' of Spiritual gifts: edification, clarification, signification, interpretation, maturation, conviction, organization."

15. The Gospel; Resurrection; All things put under Christ; Resurrection body.

    "Death swallows us, but resurrection swallows death." v. 54-55

    "The believer must be still standing, but not standing still." v. 58

16. Sunday offerings; Opportunities and adversaries; Addicted to the ministry.

    "Giving should be done responsively, systematically, individually, deliberately, proportionately and voluntarily." v. 1-2

II CORINTHIANS

1. Comfort and consolation; Apostolic ministry with simplicity and sincerity.

    "You cannot encourage someone unless you know something about discouragement." - Ed Gibson v. 4-10

2. Reclaim the wayward; Unforgiveness – a device of Satan; We are a savor.

"If a soul is worth saving, it's worth reclaiming." v. 8

"The Devil uses doubt, discouragement, deceit, discord and despair against believers." v. 11

"God wants the world to know Him by showing them us." v. 14-16

3. Ye are our epistle; The ministration of the Spirit brings liberty and understanding.

4. We have this ministry, this treasure, this faith; Light affliction-weight of glory.

5. Earthly and heavenly house; Judgment Seat of Christ; Terror of Lord; Love of Christ.

6. Approved by suffering; Be not unequally yoked with unbelievers.

7. We have defrauded no man; Godly sorrow worketh repentance; Joy of Titus.

8. Liberal giving of Macedonians; Proves love, gives equality; Accountability of messenger.

"The cross is our example and pattern for giving." v. 8,9

9. Give bountifully, not grudgingly; Grace to the giver; the unspeakable gift.

"God loveth a cheerful giver, but He will even take it from a grouch."
- Cham McMillen v. 7

10. Weapons of our warfare; Comparing ourselves, not wise; Let God commend us.

11. Paul's jealousy that they not believe another gospel; List of Paul's sufferings.

12. Out-of-the-body experience; Thorn in the flesh; Signs of an apostle.

"God's grace goes deeper than my grief." - Cham McMillen   v. 9

"In suffering, God gives us grace to make it,
strength to take it and power to prove it." v. 9

"Like Paul, each believer needs to learn to adorn the thorn." v. 7-10

"Our job as Christians is to make Jesus look good." v. 20-21

13. Examine yourselves; Warning to do right in truth; Farewell.

GALATIANS

1. Another gospel; Paul's call and gospel not of men but of God.

2. Paul, apostle to the Gentiles; Peter rebuked for dissembling; Crucified with Christ.

3. Justified by faith, not works, law or flesh like Abraham; Law is schoolmaster.

"The Law cannot give life,
it is there to bring us to Christ."   v. 21,24

4. In the fullness of time; Paul travailed till Christ be formed in them; Two sons and two covenants.

5. Stand fast in liberty; Works of the flesh; Fruit of the Spirit.

6. Restore in meekness; Bear burdens; I will glory in the cross, bear His marks.

EPHESIANS

1. Spiritual blessings in heavenly places; Paul's prayer for them.

2. We are quickened, raised, saved, workmanship, made nigh, built together.

> *"Be a risk-taker, not a caretaker,*
> *lest you become an undertaker."* v. 10

3. Mystery – Gentiles are fellow-heirs; In Christ - boldness, access, strength.

4. Unity among believers; Gift to perfect the saints; Putting Off and Putting On.

> *"You become what you are committed to."* v. 1

5. Children, live clean; Understand God's will; Wives and Husbands.

> *"It is impossible to whine and sing at the same time."* v. 19

6. Children, Fathers, Servants; The Christian's Armor.

> *"Internal discouragement will cause external defeat."* v. 10-18

PHILIPPIANS

1. Bonds are for the furtherance of the gospel; I will continue for your furtherance.

> *"Don't ask how can I get out of this problem,*
> *ask what can I learn from it."* Phil. 1:12-18

2. Have unity; Kenosis; Work out the work in you; Timothy and Epaphroditus.

3. No confidence in the flesh; Forgetting, reaching, pressing; Beware of false teachers.

4. Stand fast; Same mind; Prayer and peace; Think on these things; contentment.

"When giving to the Lord, Faith it in." - Cham McMillen   v. 19

COLOSSIANS

1. What we have in Christ; What Christ is to us; What He did for us; Christ in you.

"We will have revival if Jesus has no rival."
- Luke Knickerbocker v. 18

2. Christ is all I need: not legalism, or intellectualism, mysticism, asceticism.

*"Everything we need for the journey to Glory
is found in Jesus, our Treasure Chest."* v. 3

3. Seek, set affection on heavenly; Mortify members; Put off and put on; Wives and husbands.

4. Continue in prayer, your walk and speech; Greetings from the brethren.

I THESSALONIANS

1. This church became followers of Christ, examples to others, and witnesses to all.

2. Paul's pure, unblamable ministry among them; They suffered persecution; Satan hindered.

3. Timothy sent to encourage them; He reported their faithfulness to Paul.

4. Teaching on sanctification, honest labor, rapture of church.

5. Day of the Lord; Let us watch, be respectful, mindful, thankful, careful, faithful.

"If we were sold on the act of praying, we would rarely stop praying."
- Norman Stevens v. 17

II THESSALONIANS

1. A growing faith and charity; Revelation of Christ in judgment; Glorify God.

"You can give without loving, but you cannot love without giving." v. 3

2. Tribulation Antichrist; Strong delusion; Stand fast and hold the traditions.

3. Pray for us; Withdraw from disorderly (lazy) brethren to shame them.

I TIMOTHY

1. Paul exhorts Timothy to correct those who teach false doctrine; God changed Paul.

"If you don't live it, you don't understand it." v. 7

2. Pray for kings; One God and one mediator; Modest women, under authority.

3. Qualifications for a bishop, deacons and wives; God manifest in the flesh.

4. Doctrines of devils in latter times; Let no man despise thy youth; Heed doctrine.

"Fear gives us a reason to trust." v. 10

5. Treatment of elders, women, widows; Double honor; Keep yourself pure.

6. Christian servants and masters; Godliness with contentment; Love of money;

"Flee, follow, fight."

"Complacency is being satisfied with self; contentment is being satisfied with God." - Bobby Robertson v. 6-8

"Covet not cash but character." v. 10-11

"Praying for the flock will keep you from playing with the flock." v. 10-12

II TIMOTHY

1. Timothy's faith from his mother and grandmother; Be not ashamed of Paul's chains; Sound words.

"The man of God ought to be a godly man." v. 9

2. Striving and suffering; Study to rightly divide truth; Shun babblings; Strive not.

"If no cross-bearing, then no crown-wearing." v. 11-12

3. Signs of perilous times; Form of godliness; Godly will suffer persecution; Inspiration.

"Faith without a promise is like feet without a world to stand on." v. 9,10

4. Preach the Word; I am ready, I have fought, I have finished the course, I have kept faith; Demas and Mark.

"Preaching comforts the afflicted and afflicts the comfortable." II Tim. 4:2

"Sermons ought to be Scriptural, interesting, timely, challenging, compassionate, authoritative, informative, encouraging and Christ-centered." - James Hall v. 2

"In running life's course, you may not win,
but you must finish." v. 7

"Paul left Timothy a charge, a caution, a course and a crown."
v. 1-8 -Gene Reynolds

"If your faith falters before the finish, it was faulty from the first."
- J.D. Grush v. 10

"In ten years, you will be the same person plus the books
you have read and the people you have met."
- Don Strange II Tim. 4:13

TITUS

1. Qualifications for elders; Exhort and rebuke Jewish gainsayers, lazy Cretans.

2. Teach sound doctrine to men, women, young women, servants; Blessed hope.

3. Subject to rulers; Meek unto all; Not of works are ye saved; Reject heretics.

PHILEMON

1. Paul pleads the case of Onesimus, Philemon's runaway, but redeemed slave.

HEBREWS

1. Jesus, as God the Son, is better than the angels; Is Creator of all.

2. Jesus' suffering, servitude, subjection qualifies Him as faithful High Priest.

3. Jesus is greater than Moses; Today, harden not your heart.

4. Enter into His rest; Word of God is quick…; Hold fast, come boldly in prayer.

   "Presumption is the high road to ruin." - Matthew Henry   v. 1

5. An High Priest after the order of Melchisedec; Discernment – milk or meat.

6. Go on to perfection; He cannot lie because of his counsel and oath; better salvation.

7. Abraham and Melchizedek; Jesus greater than Levitical priesthood: six reasons.

8. A better New Covenant: It is fixed, heavenly form, faultless, of faith.

   "The Law is strong enough to condemn
   but not strong enough to save."   v. 13

9. Jesus is better than Tabernacle, high priest, animal blood; Appointed once to die.

   "We cannot live without blood, without faith and without holiness."
   9:22;11:6;12:14

10. Jesus' offering and sacrifice better than Old Testament ones; Not forsaking church assembly.

   "The church is your spiritual gas station." v. 24-25

   "Spiritual food depends on a spiritual appetite (Word),
   A spiritual appetite depends on a spiritual atmosphere (Church).
   A spiritual atmosphere must be chosen." v.22-25

11. Definition of faith; Hall of Faith; They received promises but we experience the fulfillment.

"FAITH - Forsaking All, I Trust Him." v. 1

"Faith is believing in something to the point where you will trust it." v. 2

"Faith is not a destination, but a daily walk." Joe Elwell v. 5

"Noah's stock was riding high, when the rest of the world was in liquidation." v. 7

"The enemy was behind Israel in the Red Sea and before them in the Jordan." v.29-30

12. Run the race; Chastening; Esau rejected; Believers like Abel; God is a consuming fire.

"A good thing is a bad thing if it keeps you from the best things." v. 1

13. Remember the brethren; Remember, obey, salute those who rule over you.

"Moral honor leads to marital contentment." v. 4

JAMES

1. Trying of faith; Enduring temptation; Doers, not hearers only; True religion.

"Positive thinkers don't believe in Heaven unless it's for everybody and they don't believe in Hell unless it's for nobody." v. 8

"Our righteousness is from God; our religion is for man." v. 26-27

2. Respect of persons; Faith without works is dead; Ex. – Abraham, Rahab.

   "If God gives you Paul's faith, you will soon have James' works." v. 17

   "Any faith that does not change one's life is a dead faith." v. 17

   "Faith justifies us before God; works justify us before men." v. 22

3. Power of the tongue: fire, poison; God's wisdom is pure, peaceable, without partiality.

   *"Your walk talks and your talk talks,
   but your walk talks louder than your talk talks."* v. 13

4. Wars: self, world; Submit, draw nigh, humble; Speak no evil; If the Lord will.

   "There are wars among us, because of wars within us." v. 1-2

   *"We can be too big for God to use,
   but we can never be too small."* v. 10

   "Pride is depending on self instead of God." v. 13-17

5. Woe to rich; Be patient unto Christ's coming; To the sick: pray, confess.

I PETER

1. We are elect, kept; Trial of faith; Be holy; Incorruptible inheritance.

2. As newborn babes, as lively stones; Chosen generation, submit to government; In His steps.

   "Ignorance and foolishness is a dangerous combination." v. 15

   *"Jesus is the Sin-bearer (Savior), the Burden-bearer (Comforter),
   the Deed-bearer (of earth and heaven)"* v. 24

3. Relationships of wives and husbands; Unity among believers; Suffering with a good conscience.

4. Strangers to this world; Do not think trials as strange; Judgment begins at the House of God.

> *"Don't get cold feet in the fire of trials."* v. 12

5. To elders: feed the flock, be example; Younger, submit; Be vigilant against the Devil.

II PETER

1. Precious faith; Precious promises; Witness of His majesty; More sure word of prophecy.

> *"There are no precious promises without the precious faith."* v. 1-3

> *"The authority of the Word is more sure than an eyewitness account."* v. 18-21

2. False prophets: heresies, covetousness, despise government, immoral; like dogs and pigs.

> *"The punishment of sinners in former ages is for the example of us who come after."* v. 4-9

3. Scoffers: deny creation, Flood; God's judgment of fire; Holiness enjoined.

I JOHN

1. Life and fellowship in Jesus; If we say we have no sin; If we confess our sins.

> *"As believers, we have sin in us, but no sin on us."* v. 8-10

2. Love God, the brethren; Love not the world; Ye have an unction, an anointing, and an abiding.

"The Contemporary Church has contemporary music,
has a contemporary dress code, has a contemporary preacher
with a contemporary message."
- Ray Hancock v.15-17

3. Now we are sons of God; Love in deed and truth; Obedience brings answers to prayer.

4. Try the spirits; God is love, love one another; Perfect love casts out fear.

5. Overcomers; Trinity; Eternal security; Confidence in prayer; All unrighteousness is sin.

   "It is not the commitment of sin that makes a man unsaved;
   it is the commitment to sin." v. 18

II JOHN

1. Walk in truth, in love; Beware of deceivers; Doctrine of Christ determines truth.

   "Love will avail where commandments will not." v. 5

III JOHN

1. Walking in truth.

   "Gaius, the encourager; Diotrophes, the dictator;
   Demetrius, the example" - Tom Sexton

JUDE

1. Contend for the faith; Judged: ungodly angels, Sodom and Gomorrah, Cain, Balaam and Korah.

"Christians are preserved , not pickled." v. 1

"You will never have compassion for the lost until you first have a passion for God." v. 20-23

REVELATION

1. Vision of Jesus; Alpha and Omega; Seven stars (pastors); Seven candlesticks (churches).

2. Message to pastor of Ephesus, to Smyrna, to Pergamos, to Thyatira.

"Believers often substitute being with Jesus with doing for Jesus." v. 2-4

3. Message to pastors of Sardis, to Philadelphia, to Laodicea.

4. Glimpse of God; Seven Spirits of God; Four beasts; Twenty-four elders; All praise God.

5. Lamb only worthy to open book; Worthy is the Lamb by angels, elders, beasts.

6. First seal - white horse; Second seal - red horse; Third seal - black horse; Fourth seal - pale horse; Fifth seal - souls slain; Sixth seal - earthquake.

7. Four angels; 144,000 sealed of Israel; Martyrs from Tribulation worship and praise.

8. Seventh seal - silence; First Trumpet - one-third grass burned; Second Trumpet - one-third sea blood; Third trumpet - wormwood; Fourth trumpet - one-third sky darkened.

9. Fifth trumpet - five months locust torment; Sixth trumpet - army of 200 million kill one-third of men; Man refuses to repent.

10. Christ, mighty angel, stands on land and sea; John eats little book to learn the prophecy.

11. Two Witnesses; Great earthquake; Seventh trumpet - worship; Temple open; hail, earthquake.

12. Woman, her child and the dragon; brethren overcome Satan; Woman delivered.

13. Beast, Dragon, false prophet; Image of the Beast, number of the Beast, 666.

14. Lamb with 144,000; Judgment on Babylon and Mark-takers; Winepress of blood.

15. Sea of glass with saints harping and singing; Preparation for seven angels with seven vials.

16. First vial - sores; Second vial - bloody sea; Third vial - waters bloody; Fourth vial - sun scorches men; Fifth vial - darkness; Sixth vial - Armegeddon; Seventh vial - great earthquake.

17. Great Whore; Religious mystery Babylon riding Beast; Is destroyed by Beast.

18. Political Babylon destroyed; Nations mourn; Believers rejoice.

19. Four Allelujahs; Marriage supper of the Lamb; Jesus wars with the beast and false prophet.

20. Devil bound 1,000 years; Jesus reigns 1,000 years; Gog and Magog; Great White Throne Judgment.

21. New heaven and earth; River of life, tree of life, no night; New Jerusalem.

22. "I come quickly."; Warning concerning changing God's Word; Invitation to come to Christ.

Books by Thomas Knickerbocker

The Great Experiment (biography of Tom's parents:
David and Lois Knickerbocker)

God's Design for Music

God's Design for Clothing

Biblical Design for Ministry

God's Design for Marriage

Christian, Be a Newspaper Columnist

Around the World in 80 Ways

Reaching the Nations with the Nationals
(History, Polices and Practices of HELP Ministries)

Songs that Strengthen the Soul
(Song book of 80 original songs
also recorded on 3 CD's)

Art of Taking an Established Church